Hollywood on the Spot

Hollywood on the Spot

Crimes Against the Early Movie Stars

PATRICK DOWNEY

ISBN: 1518641628
ISBN 13: 9781518641626

For the Usual Suspects,
life is good

Contents

Preface

L ike many fans of old Hollywood, my first trip into the dark side of Tinseltown was via *Hollywood Babylon* by Kenneth Anger. Since the publication of that tome, there has been no shortage of books on the subjects of crime and scandal during the early days of the movie colony. So what makes this book different from all the others? It is the aim of the author to introduce you to, not necessarily the offences that the stars themselves may have committed, but the crimes against the stars that have thus far gone unreported, or, if they have been discussed, to go more in depth and tell the full story. Readers will notice that certain crimes are omitted: namely, the murder of William Desmond Taylor and the death of producer Thomas Ince, whose untimely demise is sometimes chalked up to homicide. Both of these accounts have been examined in numerous other volumes and there is nothing new that this author can add. Therefore, forcing the reader to slog through a rehashing of these stories for the simple sake of inclusion seems unnecessary.

However, speaking of Ince, the one attempted murder of a movie star uncovered while researching this book was the almost-assassination of Ince's Hollywood friend Marion Davies. As Christmas 1931 was approaching, Marion began to receive numerous packages at her Santa Monica home. On the seventeenth of December a box arrived showing what turned out to be a fictitious return address from Malibu, California. It joined the pile with all the others. Four days later Marion asked her butler to open it.

Inside was a package with a message written on it that it was for Marion only. The butler unwrapped the gift and there was a box and a key. When he inserted the key into the box it began to smoke. Correctly assuming that something was amiss, the butler ran it outside. The police were called, and they let it soak in water for a number of hours. The box turned out to be a homemade bomb containing twenty lead slugs, which, if they didn't kill Marion outright, would have at the very least disfigured her.

For the most part, stars of the early years didn't have to worry about murder; robbery, in its many different forms, however, was another thing. Because newspapers and fan magazines were always broadcasting how much a movie star or director earned each week, Hollywood personalities became prime targets for anyone looking to make an easy buck. The stars constantly had to be on guard as to who might try to take advantage of them; not all thieves came wearing masks and carrying guns. Many stars were routinely ripped off in the daily running of their lives. A good example is actor Richard Arlen who, circa 1933, was averaging a monthly grocery bill of roughly $260. (Adjusted for inflation, that is equivalent to just under $4,700 in 2015 dollars.) Richard felt he was being fleeced because the grocer knew he was a movie star. For an experiment he had his secretary do the grocery shopping for a month. The bill fell to seventy-three dollars (roughly $1,300 in 2015). Sometimes the household staff was involved in the theft, helping to pad the bills and splitting the proceeds with the butcher, baker, florist, or whatever supplier/service provider was used. Department stores' salespeople, doctors, dentists, plumbers: movie people had to be cautious of them all.

Not all crimes against the movie colony were of the non-threatening, bill-padding, or overcharging sort. Straight-up armed robbery, burglary, extortion, and threats of kidnapping were also a constant strain on Tinseltown's famous, and those are the stories that this book seeks to tell. Following are some of the more infamous accounts regarding crimes committed against the stars, spanning Hollywood's golden years of the mid-1920s through the 1930s.

One

The Plot to Kidnap America's Sweetheart

A Rolls-Royce roadster raced down Sunset Boulevard; at the wheel, perspiration on his forehead and a grim look on his face, was action film star Douglas Fairbanks. In the passenger seat sat his wife, the world-famous movie star dubbed, "America's Sweetheart," Mary Pickford. Between them lay a sawed-off, double-barrel shotgun; next to that was a .45. The reason for the firepower was because, earlier that month, in May of 1925, the police had informed Hollywood's golden couple that a gang of kidnappers were planning to snatch Mary and hold her for a $200,000 ransom.

The kidnappers had been staking out the Pickford-Fairbanks movie studio for a few weeks. Doug had seen them loitering out front numerous times, and they had followed Mary home in the evenings. For weeks the police had been waiting for the gang to make a move on Mary so that they could move in and arrest them, but so far they hadn't attempted anything. Though Mary was somewhat frightened, the stress weighed heavier on Doug. Armed detectives guarded their house, an armed guard shadowed Mary at the studio, and each evening an armed escort followed them home from the studio.

As they left the studio that evening, Doug's eyes darted about looking for the car of detectives that was supposed to follow them home. No cars pulled out behind them, but Mary noticed a convertible, top up, driving in front of them with some men gazing at her from the rear window. She brought it to Doug's attention.

"I'll keep my eye on it, Mary," he said. "How about the police car? Do you see it anywhere?"

Mary looked about and replied in the negative. Where was their escort? His nerves already on edge, Doug studied the convertible and became convinced that it contained the kidnappers. He stepped on the accelerator and began to gain on the convertible. Mary told him not to pass them, but Doug either didn't hear or ignored her.

In 1925 Sunset Boulevard was a four-lane highway; two lanes headed east and two lanes headed west, with a grass divider. The Fairbankses were heading west in the passing lane. Destination—their home in Beverly Hills. Doug hit eighty miles per hour, bringing them up alongside the convertible. Afraid that the men might open fire as they passed, Doug said,

"If the shooting starts, Mary, drop to the floor of the car."

Mary assured Doug she would do just that but actually had no intention of hitting the deck. If it came to a fight, she would wield the .45. When it came to guns, Mary was no slouch. She had hit bull's-eyes from as far away as 150 yards. She was confident that, if it came down to a shootout, she could pick off the driver of the convertible as they sped past.

Doug zipped past the convertible, as well as the Ford that was driving in front of it. He cut across the lanes, almost causing the Ford to crash, and pulled into the parking lot of the Beverly Hills Hotel. Once in the parking lot Doug slammed on the brakes. In moments, the convertible was upon them. Grabbing the shotgun, Doug jumped from the roadster and raised it at the strangers, who pulled up behind them.

"Throw up your hands!" Fairbanks demanded.

It could have been a scene from a movie: speeding cars, guns, evil men wanting to harm America's Sweetheart, but it was all real. The events leading up to this dramatic confrontation had begun early the previous month.

Hollywood on the Spot

On April 6, 1925, two days before her thirty-third birthday, Mary Pickford began filming a picture entitled *Little Annie Rooney*. Though closer to middle-age than her teen years, Mary would play the adolescent of the title role. Occasionally over the years the internationally famous actress tried to branch out and play "woman" roles, but the results were always the same: bad box office.

Little Annie Rooney takes place on New York City's Lower East Side and involves both police and gangsters. Little did Mary know, as she was filming in the safe confines of her studio with the make-believe bad men, that real-life hoodlums were kicking around a plan to kidnap her.

The kidnap gang was made up of four men: Charles Z. Stevens (called Steve by his cohorts), who worked as a car salesman at a Hudson dealership; Claude Holcomb, a former member of a defunct Hollywood robbery gang, who was known as "Fat" to his colleagues; truck driver A.J. "Jimmy" Woods; and Louis Geck, a San Quentin parolee who did time for complicity in a murder. Geck's and Stevens's relationship went back to 1917 when they were friends in Tyrone, New Mexico. By 1922 Stevens, Geck, and Holcomb were together in Tampico, New Mexico, before moving to El Paso, Texas, and finally ending up in Los Angeles.

For two years Stevens talked about kidnapping somebody, and after months of talk it was time to put words into action. They discussed snatching child actors Jackie Coogan and "Baby" Peggy; Pola Negri came up as a possible target, but then they narrowed it down to the grandchildren of Los Angeles oil magnate Edward Doheny, and Mary Pickford. As Mary worked on *Little Annie Rooney*, the kidnappers began scoping out the Doheny mansion trying to formulate a plan to snatch the children, or at least one of his granddaughters. They went so far as to even follow them to church.

Using his Hudson automobile, Stevens drove Holcomb out to the Doheny estate on a reconnaissance mission. They parked the car and took a walk to look over the grounds. The duo were noticed by two of Doheny's employees who acted as both groundskeepers and guards. The guards didn't think much of it at first because their boss had been involved in the infamous Teapot Dome scandal, so it wasn't uncommon to have curious people stop and look the house over. The next day, however, the employees recognized Stevens and Holcomb again as they circled the house numerous times. Another time the groundskeepers saw the men circling the estate in a Ford. Assuming something was amiss, the employees went to the police and reported the incident.

The next day a detective was sent to stake out the Doheny home. Sure enough, the Hudson showed up. The groundskeepers/guards motioned to the detective that that was the car, and the detective tailed it back to the Hudson dealership. A quick run of the license proved that the car owner was Charles Stevens, occupation Hudson salesman. The detective took this info to his chief and surmised that, as a salesman, Stevens took prospective buyers out for a test drive and headed to the Doheny place and back. Since Doheny's mansion, because of the infamous history of its owner, was somewhat of a tourist destination, the detective assumed that the daily visits in the Hudson were simply Stevens trying to sell his cars, giving customers a short test drive to view a notable place and then back to the agency to talk business. The chief of detectives, George Home, however, wasn't so sure. Why would Stevens keep taking the same guy out? And why did they use a Ford on one of the trips? The chief decided to put Detective Harry Raymond on the case full time.

As the Los Angeles police were getting interested in Stevens and his yet unknown confederate, the fledgling kidnappers had decided against snatching Doheny's grandchildren. Unbeknownst to the police the gang had decided that of all the Hollywood stars they considered kidnapping, Mary would be the best option, as she probably had the most money. Not only were she and her husband both superstars as well as movie producers, Mary also owned, as they read in the papers, two million dollars-worth of Liberty Bonds.

His first morning on the case, Detective Raymond drove to the Hudson agency and began a stakeout. At around closing time, the sedan with the two men inside pulled out. Raymond assumed that the Hudson would be heading for the Doheny place so was perplexed when they turned onto Santa Monica Boulevard and headed in the direction of the movie studios.

The detective's curiosity was piqued when the Hudson pulled up in front of the Pickford-Fairbanks Studio. He drove a half block further and pulled over. For two hours he sat watching the Hudson. As the sun began to set, the front gates to the studio opened and a Rolls-Royce roadster emerged. Though she was wearing her driving goggles, Raymond immediately realized it was Mary Pickford behind the wheel. As Mary turned west onto Santa Monica Boulevard and headed towards Beverly Hills and Pickfair, the couple's home, the Hudson pulled away from the curb and followed her. Detective Raymond tailed the Hudson. The Hudson followed Mary for a number of blocks before turning off. Following the car, Raymond noted that after a short time it pulled over and the passenger got out. Stevens then went straight home.

Early the next morning Detective Raymond was staking out Stevens's house. At around six a.m. Stevens's garage opened and the salesman backed out in a Ford coupe. A few minutes later he pulled over and, after a bit, his passenger from the day before walked up and got into the car. Raymond followed them out to Beverly Hills and saw them pull off to the side of a road not far from Pickfair. Detective Raymond drove by and turned around about a half a mile away. A few minutes later the roar of Mary's Rolls-Royce engine could be heard. She zipped by Raymond and moments later Stevens and his accomplice, who pulled out after her.

Stevens followed Mary right to the studio and passed her as she entered the gate. A few blocks away Stevens drew to the curb and his friend got out. Knowing Stevens already, Detective Raymond followed the friend to his apartment at 8510 Morton Avenue, where he learned that the guy was known as "Claude Arthur." Raymond kept his eye on the apartment, and after about an hour Claude reappeared and walked to a drug store, where he made a phone call. After the call he went outside and waited. A few minutes later the Hudson sedan pulled up, only this time there was a third man in the passenger seat. Getting a good look inside the car, Raymond recognized the new man, Louis Geck, recently paroled from San Quentin after having been sent up for his part in a murder. Claude got into the car and Raymond followed them to a trucking company in the nearby town of Alhambra, where they spent ten minutes speaking with a truck driver before returning downtown.

Now that a convicted murderer was involved, a call was placed to the Pickford-Fairbanks Studio. The Chief of Detectives identified himself and, without giving away any pertinent information, learned that Mary would be leaving the studio at around eight p.m. Raymond was dispatched to make sure she got home safely. That night, around nine, Mary, still unaware that anything was wrong, pulled out of the studio and headed home, not realizing that the headlights behind her belonged to a Los Angeles detective charged with her safety. After she pulled into Pickfair, Raymond pulled up and two men stepped out of the shadows, fellow detectives assigned to guard the actress's house. They informed Raymond that he should get back to town and see the chief.

Earlier that evening while Detective Raymond was waiting at the Pickford-Fairbanks Studio, the Chief of Detectives had some men go out and pick up Louis Geck. Once in custody, and with no desire to go back to San Quentin, Geck opened up. He said that Stevens and Claude Arthur (whose real last name was Holcomb) were planning on snatching Mary. He also stated that he had no intention of going along with it, he just wanted "to see how far they would go." To prove he was on the level with the cops he agreed to set up his confederates.

Now that the police knew what was going on and who was involved in the conspiracy, it was time to contact the Fairbankses. Exactly how they were informed is in question. Doug would later testify that they were at home when he received the call. Chief Home remembered that he called Doug but did not state whether he called Pickfair or the studio. In her memoirs Mary would write that the call was placed to Doug at the studio and he called her at Pickfair, where she was enjoying a rare day off.

"Mary, where are you?" Doug asked when Mary answered the phone.

"I'm rowing down Hollywood Boulevard in a golden gondola," Mary quipped back, thinking it was obvious where she was since she answered the phone.

"This is serious, Mary," Doug said. "What part of the house are you in?"

"The upper hall," Mary replied.

"All right. Now listen carefully," Doug continued, "Call the butler and the gardener and tell them not to leave the house. Go immediately to your own room and lock the door. Do you hear?"

"Yes, Douglas, but what's it all about?" Mary inquired.

"I can't explain now. I'm leaving the studio and coming right out. Please do as I say."

A short time later Doug arrived at the house with the Chief of Detectives.

"Mary," he said, "the police have just got wind of a plot to kidnap you and hold you for ransom."

Geck's confession was hardly enough evidence to put the would-be-kidnappers away, so it was determined that the only thing to do was to catch them in action. Mary and Doug would go about their business as usual as if they were unaware of any plot; however, Doug insisted that Mary have an armed guard with her at the studio at all times. It was also deemed too dangerous for Mary to travel to and from the studio alone anymore, so the detectives had a conundrum. They needed the kidnappers to make a move, but they also needed to keep Mary out of harm's way. Enter Crete Sippel. Crete was a stuntwoman who had doubled for Mary numerous times. She was summoned to the Pickford-Fairbanks Studio, where she assumed that she would be working on *Little Annie Rooney* and was surprised to arrive and be greeted by the Chief of Detectives.

The chief explained to her that she was indeed needed to double for Mary but not in the capacity she was used to. Without spilling the beans about the kidnapping, the chief explained that she would simply drive Mary's Rolls-Royce to and from the studio every day. Without giving details, he stated that the job could prove dangerous and offered her the chance to refuse. Crete accepted the job and that night, donning Mary's coat, hat, and goggles, she pulled up to the gate. "Good night, Miss Pickford," the guard yelled as he raised the gate. To make it look even more realistic, Doug Fairbanks stepped on the running board and gave her a kiss goodbye. Hitting the gas, Crete sped to Pickfair. Detectives followed her in hopes of arresting the kidnappers in action. Mary journeyed home later in a car with Doug and an armed escort. For a week this charade went on, Crete driving both to and home from the studio, but the kidnappers did not act.

Around noon on May 19, the Hudson again appeared outside the studio. Stevens and two others sat there for about an hour as the numerous employees came and went for their lunch break. At one point Stevens got out and gazed through the gate. Whenever the detectives were aware that the kidnappers were staking out the studio, a call was placed to Doug Fairbanks, who would nonchalantly walk to the front gates and observe them.

That night, with the kidnappers refusing to act, the authorities put plan B into effect. Crete was thanked for her services and sent on her way. Instead of waiting for the kidnappers to strike, the chief decided to try to procure evidence by recording a meeting. So far, however, the suspects only met in the Hudson or Ford. He wanted to get them altogether in a room where he could record their plot. Geck was called in and informed that he would be checking into the Hayward Hotel at Spring and Sixth streets. He was also told to invite is confederates over for a meeting.

Geck was given room 224 and the detectives took room 225, which was connected by an adjoining door. To insure Geck didn't run out, Detective Raymond escorted him to the furnished room he lived in and helped him pack and then took him back to the Hayward. In room 225 a number of small holes, nothing noticeable to the naked eye, were bored in the door separating the rooms. The mirrored dresser in Geck's room was moved to the far side of the wall so detectives would be able to see everything going on in the room through its reflection. There was about a quarter-inch between the floor and the door bottom connecting the rooms, so detectives had both full visual and audible contact with Geck's room. Now the detectives simply had to wait for the bad guys to show up.

It appeared that Geck had double-crossed the detectives because after May 19, neither the Hudson nor the Ford was seen at Pickfair or the studio and Geck hadn't tipped them off to any meetings. Finally, after more than a week, Geck got in touch with Detective Raymond on May 27. There was going to be a rendezvous that night. Raymond, the chief, and two stenographers took their places. The stenographers, supplied with writing pads and stethoscopes, lay on a mattress by the door with the chest piece of the medical listening device lodged at the space between the door and the floor. At eight o'clock there was a knock on Geck's door.

"Hello, Fat!" Geck said as Claude Holcomb walked in. The two men chatted. As time went on the police became frustrated as the duo talked about everything but the kidnapping. Finally Geck mentioned something about working and this triggered some dialogue that the police could use.

"I don't want a job," Fat said, "We've been planning on getting 'The Party' for the last two years. If Steve [Stevens] would put up the money I could get somebody to do it for us."

"Suppose you get her and they don't come across with the money?" Geck responded.

"I'd just keep her," Fat said.

"What would you do with her?" Geck asked.

"After going to all that trouble, we'd get the money. I may be soft about some things. But," Fat changed thoughts, "I think Steve ought to put up the money so we could pay someone to pick her up. You know, you can get fellows to do this kind of stuff when they're broke."

Geck then asked about the area where they were thinking of taking Mary captive.

"You think that neighborhood out there will be all right?" he said.

"It'll be all right." Fat said.

There was a knock at the door and they let in the truck driver from Alhambra, A.J. Woods.

"Where is your friend Stevens?" Woods asked.

"He said he'd be down soon," Geck said.

The conversation turned to holding Mary in a house after they snatched her.

"Does it make you kind of nervous?" Woods asked Fat.

"Oh, no," Fat replied, "but I don't like the idea of picking her up. That's the hard part."

"You're thinking of the pleasant end of it," Woods said. "We're going to have to rent a house. What are you going to do if Steve drops out? How much jack will it take?"

"It'll take about a hundred bucks," Fat replied. "We've got to hire a big car and rent a house."

Stevens never showed up the first night, and no more was discussed about the kidnapping. It becomes apparent when reading the transcript taken during the gang's meetings that they never really had a cohesive plan—just a lot of talk about who would do what, who didn't want to do what, and mostly questions instead of answers.

Another meeting was set up for the following night, but both Stevens and Woods were no-shows. Holcomb and Geck shot the breeze for a while before getting back to the kidnapping.

"You don't know of any other guy we could get in Steve's place if he pulls out?" Fat asked.

"I don't know of any," Geck replied.

"Jimmy [Woods] would take care of 'The Party' all right if we'd pick her up," Fat said.

"What'll we do with Douglas [Fairbanks]?" Geck asked.

"We'll have to shoot him," Fat laughed. "The money is what we're after."

"You think Jimmy will take care of 'The Party'?" Geck inquired.

"If we pick her up, he will," Fat said, "It'll be a kind of tough picking her up unless she goes out at night. At seven it isn't so dark. I don't want to pick her up. I think I'd do better taking care of her."

"Mary doesn't weigh much, does she?" Geck said.

"I guess not but that doesn't make much difference," Fat said. "She is going to raise hell when we get hold of her. She'll think it's a hold-up or something."

"What if she pulls a big .45?" Geck asked.

"Have to shoot her, that's all. No use to back out. I wouldn't hesitate to shoot."

"You wouldn't shoot a woman, would you?" Geck asked.

"I wouldn't care who it was. I'd shoot." Fat said.

"Wouldn't you rather jump off her car than take a chance of getting shot?" Geck asked.

"You're taking a chance anyway," Fat said. "Liable to get shot. I wouldn't back out. This stuff is a hard proposition. Like holding up a bank. When a fellow goes into it he has to carry it through. Like one of those guys who used to be with us. He'd shoot if a fellow didn't move when he told him to. He had an awful voice. When he told a man to put up his hands, he put 'em up. He stuck up a fellow one night and the fellow was so scared he never did report it. One day he stuck up a café a block from the Hollywood police station. He's the one I wanted to get for this job. That fellow wouldn't back out."

"Think Steve will lay down?" Geck asked.

"I don't think so," Fat responded, adding, "Anybody in that room [225] over there?"

"I never see anybody in there," Geck said, "I think they're holding it for the Shriners who are coming next week for their convention." Then, changing the topic, he added, "What amount did Jimmy agree on?"

"He said he'd be satisfied with twenty five thousand apiece, but not me."

"What do you want?"

"Fifty thousand," Fat answered. "We can get that just as easy. Those fellows would have to pay us. They wouldn't let the picture stop now."

"Fifty thousand for yourself?"

"Yes."

"That would be two hundred thousand. That's an awful lot of money." Geck said.

"Yes. It'll dig an awful hole in her bank account. She can sell some of her Liberty Bonds."

"When Mary is picked up she will get a good look at us," Geck said.

"I'll have on a chauffeur's suit and goggles. She won't know me," Fat replied.

"What could we carry the two hundred thousand in?" Geck asked.

"A handbag. She might have a little money on her. Some jewelry too," Fat said.

After that Fat said he was tired of waiting for Stevens and took off. The police were now about a month into their investigation and not much farther along than when they started. The strain was also affecting Doug and Mary, and the events of the following day would force the police to wrap things up sooner than they wanted.

On the evening of May 29, the detectives who were to escort Doug and Mary home were parked outside the studio, as were Stevens and possibly more of the kidnap team in the Ford. Mary's roadster came to the front gate with Doug at the wheel. Perhaps the kidnappers were simply timing the exit or were taken aback at seeing Doug in the driver's seat, but for some reason they pulled away. The detectives pulled out to follow them. The roadster brought up the rear. Looking out the rear window some of the officers noticed that Fairbanks seemed to be speeding up to them. For some distance the roadster gained speed before finally blowing by the detective's car. It cut off the Ford containing the kidnappers, almost causing it to crash as Doug pulled into the parking lot of the Beverly Hills Hotel. The Ford continued on its way but the detectives pulled into the parking lot. Just as they rolled to a stop the detectives found themselves staring down the barrel of Douglas Fairbanks's sawed-off shotgun.

After being told to raise their hands, the detectives quickly identified themselves and informed Doug that the Ford he cut off was the kidnappers. That was enough. Covered in sweat, his nerves rattled, Doug lost it.

"I will not subject my wife to any more of this danger," he told them, "I insist that you arrest those men immediately." He also insisted that Mary not be there when the arrests took place.

Later that night the detectives and stenographers were back in room 225 for what would be the gang's final meeting, and this time Stevens actually showed up. Drinks were served and then they got down to business; the business of talking, but not really getting any closer to making a move.

"The way I figure it out," Fat started, "is that whenever you try to pick somebody off the road in the daytime you've got to go some. At night it would be easy."

"We'll get 'The Party' and the money," Stevens replied, trying to set his confederate at ease.

"I'd rather do anything than pick up 'The Party,'" Fat said.

"Want to go out there tomorrow?" Stevens asked.

"Sure," Geck answered, adding, "What were you figuring, Steve?"

"We're figuring fifty thousand dollars apiece," Fat interjected, "Isn't that what you're figuring?"

"No, twenty-five thousand dollars," Stevens said.

"Fifty thousand. We can get that just as easy as the other," Fat countered.

"What do you say, Steve? Is it going to be one, two, or five?" Geck asked.

"We estimate two as about as much as we can get, but it's just as easy for Doug to raise five. He knows that he and Mary can start dead broke tomorrow and make plenty. He'll figure he has to do it."

"Suppose he refuses to come across?" Geck said.

"The public would never go see Doug's pictures if he didn't come across," Stevens said, "He'll come through within twenty-four hours. If he doesn't, the only thing to do is to stand pat."

"Sure, that's the only way," Fat agreed, "We want to go through with this no matter what happens. We can't run. Kill her. Make up our mind you're going so far and you can't back out."

"You must realize that if you stand pat they're going to try to make us back down. If we don't back down, they've got to come through," Stevens added.

"We're going to get the money," Fat said. "If I take care of 'The Party' she won't be turned back."

"She can't be turned back," Stevens said.

"That part don't worry me. Picking her up, that's what worries me," Fat said.

"Well, it all depends on circumstances at the time," Stevens said. "We have to get acquainted with Mary's movements. The whole thing is simply having a knowledge of conditions."

"How do you get to the Fairbanks home?" Geck asked.

"The way we went is the only way. I think we went to the end of the road. She can be picked up on the road," Stevens said.

"I don't see why we must go to the expense of a high-powered car." Geck said.

"She might step on the gas and run away from us. If she gets suspicious of you, she's gone. Of course, if I could get hold of her it wouldn't be anything. We saw her. She isn't any taller than I am." Stevens said.

"Doug isn't very tall," Fat said.

"No," Stevens responded, "but he's an athlete."

"Aw, he doesn't amount to much," Fat said.

"He'd come through with the money thinking maybe they're going to kill her. They think about those things. They don't take chances with kidnappers. No danger. They'll come through with the money." Stevens said.

"Who's going to rent the house to keep her in?" Geck asked.

"Fat is willing to drive the car if you pick her up." Stevens responded.

"I wouldn't mind renting the house," Fat stated, "But somebody's got to rent the car. I'll drive the car and I'm going to dress up like a chauffeur."

"Why not dress up like one of those Shriners?" Stevens suggested.

"That's a good idea. We could have our car all decorated," Fat agreed.

The men then formed a plan. Since there was a big Shriner convention coming to town they would dress up like Shriners, fezzes and all, and decorate their car with Shriner banners. They would force Mary's car to the side of the road and cheerfully take her from her roadster and place her in their car. If anyone saw they would simply look like a bunch of overzealous conventioneers having a bit of fun with America's Sweetheart.

After a bit more talk Fat made a statement. "We're a bunch of chumps."

"Why?" Stevens asked.

"Sitting around here waiting."

"Well, we never did have the finances, but tonight we figured out a lot of details we hadn't figured out before."

That would be the gang's final meeting. Detectives had been trailing them day and night for a month, and other than coming up with the Shriner routine, they weren't any closer to pulling the job than they were at the beginning of May. No safe house had been rented to confine Mary in while waiting for the ransom. No car with a high-powered engine had been purchased. After the run-in with Doug earlier in the evening, Chief Home decided it was time to pick them up.

The following day, as they did so many times before, Stevens and Holcomb pulled up outside the movie studio around the lunch hour. Stevens got out and loitered near a building, watching, while Holcomb stayed in the car. Detective Raymond was on hand with some backup. According to Raymond, they simply walked up and grabbed Stevens and dragged him to the Ford where they got Holcomb before he knew what was happening. Mary's version was a bit different. Though she didn't witness the event, she learned firsthand from her husband and some others who were on hand to see it. According to her account, Detective Raymond was standing inside the studio gate with Doug and said, "Watch me slug them."

Raymond nonchalantly made his way up to the Ford and, as Mary remembered being told, bashed Holcomb across the head with his pistol butt, knocking him unconscious. The he trained his weapon on Stevens and said, "Will you take it the hard way or will you come quietly?"

After the men were cuffed and in the car, Raymond pulled up to the studio gate to chat with Doug and the others. While conversing, Raymond pulled out a pouch of tobacco and rolled himself a cigarette with one hand. Doug took notice that the detective's hand wasn't shaking a bit. Afterwards, Doug found Mary inside the studio and told her the ordeal was over. Mary, according to her memoir, "...*amazed myself and him (Doug) by breaking down completely. I suppose the tension finally snapped. I suddenly trembled all over and had myself a good hard feminine cry.*"

"THREE SEIZED IN PLOT TO KIDNAP MARY PICKFORD," the *Los Angeles Times* declared on its front page. While page one of the *Oakland Tribune* heralded, "PICKFORD ABDUCTION PLOT FOILED," the *Billings Gazette* announced, "KIDNAPERS FOILED IN PLOT TO ABDUCT 'OUR MARY'; 3 HELD". The three perpetrators all wrote confessions and across the country Americans read about how Stevens, Holcomb, and Woods had schemed to make off with their sweetheart. As a result of his assisting the police, Geck was exonerated. After a few days the stories subsided. Prosecutors began to build a case and Mary went back to work on *Little Annie Rooney*, which wrapped on June 11.

The trial began on July 24, and lasted almost three weeks. The defense attempted to have the signed confessions thrown out, stating that they were made under duress. Stevens's attorney said that his client was beaten up and received three broken ribs in attempt to get him to make a signed statement. Holcomb took the stand and described his ordeal.

"I was brought down to Chief Home's office," he said, "and Harry Raymond said to me, 'Fat, we want a statement out of you and we want to get it free and voluntarily' then he said, 'what were you doing at the studio?' I said, 'we went there with Louie [Geck] to see a friend of his about a job.' Then he struck me in the nose."

Holcomb went on to say that another detective took him to a washbowl to clean the blood off his face and coat. Then he stated that he agreed to sign a confession after Detective Raymond promised to "stump the hell" out of him every day until he signed one.

The prosecution asked the defendants what hand Raymond had used to beat them. They responded that he used his right hand and, in one instance, his knee. In response to this, prosecutors produced a photo from the day of the arrests in which Raymond was wearing a bandage on his right hand. The reason for the bandage was that three days previous to the arrests the detective slipped in the shower at the Y.M.C.A and sprained his hand. The "masseur" from the Y who had bandaged his hand took the stand and swore to the accuracy of the story. Unfortunately for the defense,

Mary's statement about Raymond knocking Holcomb unconscious during the arrests wouldn't come to light for another thirty years.

On July 28, Douglas Fairbanks made a brief appearance on the witness stand. He was called in to both identify the defendants and say that he had seen them loitering about the studio on numerous occasions. He was done in ten minutes. The following afternoon Mary was due to take the stand and what, until that time, had been an uneventful trial turned into a circus. The public knew Mary was to appear and the courtroom that normally held one hundred and fifty people was crammed with an estimated four hundred. Another five hundred lined the hallways of the building. A few minutes after 3:00p.m., Mary stepped off the elevator along with her mother, Doug, and Doug's brother, Robert. Deputy sheriffs pushed the party through the crowd to the judge's chambers. Once she arrived, the judge called a recess and a number of people made their way into the chambers to meet Mary, who reportedly shook hands and spoke with them all.

About the same time another case was going on in a courtroom across the lightwell from the chambers where Mary waited. The judge in that case called a recess. Members of the jury and spectators of the case rushed to the windows to catch a glimpse of Mary. Some even climbed out the eight-story window and walked across a narrow roof to get a closer look at the movie star. Ever pleasant, Mary went to the window and shook hands and spoke with her admirers. After a while a custodian shooed them back to their courtroom.

At approximately 4:00p.m., Mary was called to the witness stand. Dressed in a dark brown two-piece suit, matching shoes, and tan silk hose, topped off with a brown velour hat, she walked into the courtroom. Numerous people called out her name and she shook hands with admirers as she made her way down the aisle to take the stand. Her time as a witness was brief, barely ten minutes, in which she stated that she never saw the plotters at the studio and all that she knew about the conspiracy was what she had heard from Doug. She admitted that she drove a Rolls-Royce, which brought a gush from the crowd. She also stated that one time she did notice a small coupe following her. That was it. Mary was excused and, as she left, the hundreds who came by to see her filed out as well.

The trial continued for another two weeks without any fanfare. After the defense failed to get the confessions thrown out, they tried to put the blame on Geck, saying that he was the mastermind behind the plot. They also insinuated that the detectives involved in the case were behind it as well, that it was a great scheme to make themselves look good in the public's eye. The jury didn't buy it. On August 13, after four and a half hours of deliberations, both Charles Z. Stevens and Arthur Holcomb were found guilty and sentenced from ten years to life. Truck driver A.J. Woods managed an acquittal. His two cohorts appealed, a process that took about a year, but the verdict stood and they were shipped off to San Quentin in 1926. Both were paroled in 1931.

• • •

The fear of kidnapping, unfounded as it turned out, was revisited on the Fairbankses a few years later on July 24, 1931. On that summer morning, at their Brentwood home, Douglas Fairbanks Jr. was breakfasting with his wife Joan Crawford and a Hollywood pal named Allan Vincent when the doorbell rang. The maid answered the door and there stood a fellow named Clarence L. Lenhart, gasping for breath. He asked to speak to Doug. The servant asked his name but the man wouldn't give it. When asked why he needed to see Mr. Fairbanks, the man simply replied it was a matter of life and death.

Doug and Vincent went to the door and Lenhart told them that while in Texas he had overheard a gang plotting to kidnap both Doug and Joan and force the movie studios to pay a large ransom. The gang, Lenhart, continued, found out that he was privy to their plans so they made him an offer he couldn't refuse: join us or die. According to Lenhart, the gang took the train to Los Angeles where he managed to sneak away and come to warn them. All through his narrative Lenhart appeared frightened and informed Fairbanks that his, Lenhart's, life was now forfeit for warning him. Doug figured him to be a crank looking for a handout, but Joan and their friend Allan thought otherwise and opted to call the police. Lenhart wanted to leave because he feared that even if he were in police custody, the kidnap gang would still manage to get him before the police had a chance to round them up. Doug and Allan managed to keep him there until the police arrived.

The police investigated Lenhart and found out he did come in from Texas as he said, but they found no sign of a gang. Lenhart took them to an abandoned house that he said was to be used to hold the two stars, but there were no signs that anyone had been there or was planning to be there. After a few days they let Lenhart go and called the kidnapping plot a farce. A short time later Doug Jr. received a call at home. It was Lenhart. He told the actor that the gang had traced him to where he lived and stole all his belongings—could Mr. Fairbanks find it in his heart to give him enough money to buy a new outfit? No, he could not. Mr. Fairbanks hung up, satisfied that his first impression that the whole thing was a hoax had been validated.

Though her husband didn't believe in a plot, Joan did. Perhaps she was simply nervous about the whole ordeal, but she reportedly said that in the weeks following she felt that she was being watched and one evening she arrived home from the MGM studios declaring that a car had followed her all the way from Culver City back to Brentwood. To play it safe, Joan was given a bodyguard and she and Doug Jr. moved into a hotel for a time. "It makes me feel silly," Joan said of the ordeal, "but I'm more than ever convinced that that unknown man saved me from the horror of having my husband kidnapped or being kidnapped myself. I only hope he has got safely into hiding and that the gang will never find him to carry out its death threat." Doug's friend Allan Vincent also believed Lenhart, stating, "If it wasn't [real], that man was one of the greatest actors of criminal parts this country has ever seen and he ought to make a fortune on the screen."

• • •

Another of the silver screen's leading ladies to receive a kidnap scare was Ann Harding. Towards the end of 1931 Harding was filming a movie called *Prestige*, which would open in January 1932. Part of the production was to be filmed in Mexico so Harding, director Tay Garnett, and six others prepared to fly south of the border. Just prior to leaving, word reached them that a contingent of American kidnappers were awaiting her arrival to put the snatch on her. Another part of the gang was supposed to follow her down in another plane. According to the story the kidnappers reasoned that it would be easier to abduct and hide her in Mexico than the United States. They also reasoned that if her husband, actor Harry Bannister, didn't pony up the ransom, then her studio, RKO-Pathe, would because they had already pre-sold the movie to theaters. The flight was called off and nothing more was heard of the kidnappers.

The plot to kidnap Mary Pickford ushered in a new era for Hollywood, an era of fear. Stars no longer felt safe, nor were they. In the following decade the threat of kidnapping, extortion, and robbery were a constant amongst the movie colony's actors, directors, and producers, and most all employed private security to guard themselves and their children. Mary Pickford probably summed it up for all of Tinseltown when she wrote, *"The experience left me more cautious than it found me. We now have watchmen day and night, together with every possible police protection—and, I might add, a squad of well-trained watchdogs at Pickfair."*

Charles Stevens, ring leader of Mary Pickford kidnap gang.

Chief Home (L) questions Claude Holcomb (R) as Detective Raymond looks on.

Mary Pickford takes the stand.

Douglas Fairbanks at the trial of Mary's would-be kidnappers.

Two

Stick 'Em Up

"It happened once to me that I was robbed," Mae West told a biographer nearly fifty years after the fact. "I was sitting in my car and an armed man asked me for my jewels and my money. I turned over about a thousand dollars in cash. I wasn't giving up my life for paper money, which is interchangeable, and I knew I could always earn more.

"My diamonds, that was another story. Until that moment, I thought I knew what I'd do. I'd refuse. Even if it would have cost my life. But what are you gonna do?...I decided it was stupid to be brave. Maybe the police could get my diamonds back, but they couldn't get my life back." Mae went on to say that she saved a diamond necklace by letting it fall into her bust. She also said that the robbers only had time to spend five hundred of the thousand dollars taken before they were caught. Most of what she said was either purposely fabricated or simply a result of poor memory.

At the time of the robbery Mae wasn't yet a household name, though she had known much success in the theater and vaudeville. She came to Los Angeles in January 1932 at the behest of her old pal George Raft to appear in his newest film, *Night After Night*. On September 27, 1932, a week before the film opened, Mae's limousine was involved in an accident. Enter Harry Voiler. Mae had known Harry for a couple of years and considered him a friend. Originally from Chicago, Harry had ties to the underworld. When New York City nightclub owner Tex Guinan closed up shop in Manhattan and moved to Chicago to open a new speakeasy, she hired Harry to be her manager and see that the local gangsters were kept satisfied. Authorities closed the place in 1930 after Harry was involved in a shooting. Tex's next place was raided on New Year's Eve 1931 and, like Mae, she headed west in early 1932 in search of celluloid gold with Voiler in tow.

Following the car accident Harry offered his services to Mae and her manager James Timoney, which they graciously accepted. That night Mae, Voiler, and Timoney went out to dinner. On the way Mae asked Voiler to pull over so she could go into a store. Timoney complained that he didn't want to wait for two hours to get dinner. Mae said she'd only be ten minutes, but he didn't believe her. "I then made a proposition to Jim and Mr. Voiler," Mae would later state. "I said I'd pay them each a dollar for every minute over ten that I kept them waiting. They said it was a bet, so I went into the shop." Mae returned twenty-six minutes later and each man demanded his sixteen dollars. Mae opened her purse to pay and in doing so produced a wad of $3,400 in cash. "I counted the money in their presence and explained that I'd been carrying it with me for a day or so as I had a certain obligation to meet," Mae said.

Knowing that Mae was carrying $3,400 in cash and was always draped in thousands of dollars-worth of jewelry was too much temptation for a lifelong criminal like Voiler to resist. On the morning of September 28, Voiler dropped Mae at the studio. Later that afternoon he came across an underworld sort he'd known for some years named Edward Friedman who was killing time with a hoodlum pal from Detroit named Morris Cohen. Voiler called Friedman over and asked him if he wanted to make a grand. "Okay, what is it?" Friedman inquired. "Grab Mae West's jewels," Voiler replied. Friedman asked if Cohen could be let in and Voiler agreed. Friedman and Cohen followed Voiler out to Mae's apartment, where he told the two desperadoes that he would be arriving back there at about seven that evening and that they should be waiting there to pull the job.

After the robbery the plan was to rendezvous at Rampart between Sixth and Wilshire at eleven p.m.

At around six that evening Voiler showed up at the Paramount studio to pick up Timoney and Mae. The plan was to go out to dinner, stop off at Mae's apartment to feed her pet monkey, and then head to the fights. After eating, Harry drove to Mae's place and Timoney ran up to feed the monkey. While they were waiting, Friedman, with his hat pulled down over his eyes and his coat collar up, stepped up to the car and jerked open Mae's door. With cloth covering his hand that presumably held a gun, Friedman grunted, "Come on, the poke, the purse. Hand it over." Mae handed it over.

"Now the ring."

Mae handed over her eight-carat $3,500 diamond ring.

"The bracelet, I want that too," Friedman said making a grab for the five-thousand-dollar piece of jewelry.

"You'll get it," Mae said. "Keep your paws off me."

Finally Friedman demanded and received Mae's necklace, valued at thirty-five hundred dollars. Slamming Mae's door, Friedman ordered Voiler to drive off. Friedman jumped into a coupe with Cohen at the wheel and sped off.

Mae and Voiler met Timoney in the lobby and told him what happened. Mae wanted to call the police, but Voiler advised her against it. He told Mae that chances were that the thief would contact her and try to sell the stuff back at a reasonable rate. He argued that if they went to the cops, the papers would get a hold of the story and the robbers would sell her things off and she'd never see them again. He assured Mae that he would work to get the merchandise back. Mae agreed to wait. Later that night Voiler met with Friedman and Cohen as planned and paid them off with the cash from Mae's purse. He kept the jewelry and the rest of Mae's money for himself.

The following day Timoney received a phone call telling him where he could find Mae's purse. He asked about the jewelry but was told nothing. Two weeks later Voiler called Mae and said that he had received a wire from Phoenix saying that the jewelry was there and that the robbers were ready to talk business. Mae sent Voiler to Arizona and he called her back that night saying that all her stuff was there and that the bandits were willing to sell it back for thirty-two hundred dollars.

"Thirty-two hundred! Don't be funny. I'll pay a reasonable amount and that's all," Mae responded. Voiler told the star that the robbers weren't willing to negotiate, so Mae told him to forget it. His plan had backfired, so Harry was forced to sell the jewelry elsewhere.

Shortly after this episode Mae decided it was time to go to the police. After hearing her statement, detectives questioned her about whether she thought that Voiler might have played a part in the robbery but she assured them that he was on the up-and-up and couldn't have been involved. The police weren't so sure and did a background check. It turned out that he had done time in the Michigan State Penitentiary for armed robbery and was subsequently arrested a number of times after his release in Detroit and Chicago for assault and robbery. However, since there was no evidence they couldn't make a move on him.

A number of months later there was a drive to rid Los Angeles of all underworld characters and Voiler was one of those brought in. He was held for twenty-four hours and questioned about the Mae West robbery. He denied having anything to do with the theft and offered his services to help in any way possible to get the jewels back. He was released and he returned to Chicago.

More months went by without any breaks in the case. In the autumn of 1933, over a year after the robbery, the Los Angeles Police Department put together a special squad of detectives with the objective of clearing up the unsolved crimes that were still on the books. Mae was brought in in early November and again questioned about the crime. The more detectives studied the robbery, the more they believed that Voiler was involved; unfortunately, he was still in Chicago where they couldn't touch him. Meanwhile, detectives investigated the many haunts that Voiler was known to visit, and on one trip an underworld source mentioned that Voiler was pals with local ne'er-do-well Edward Friedman. It took a few weeks but Friedman was picked up on Thanksgiving Day. Of course he denied any involvement but finally broke down and confessed [possibly with the help of some police brutality]. Friedman spilled the whole story, fingering Voiler as the brainchild of the caper as well as naming Cohen as his get-away driver.

Detectives brought Friedman over to Mae's apartment so she could identify him. When he was paraded in front of the actress she told him to pull his hat down and pull up his coat collar.

"Now let's hear you talk," she said. "Say 'hand me your poke.'"

Friedman repeated the phrase. Mae assured the detectives that Friedman was indeed the gunman. She asked to speak to Friedman alone. The detectives stepped away while Mae quizzed Friedman about Voiler's participation.

"I feel downright ill," Mae said as she rejoined the detectives. "I can hardly believe this of Harry Voiler."

On December 4, Friedman went before a Grand Jury and repeated his story, implicating both Voiler and Cohen. Mae also took the stand and described how she had paid for Voiler to fly out to Phoenix to retrieve her gems. She also told them that she hadn't suspected Harry at all. "I've known Voiler for a number of years," she told them. "He has now turned out to be a snake in the grass. I guess you might as well say he has been a friend in the grass." That night an attorney claiming to represent Harry Voiler paid Friedman a visit in jail. What the lawyer told the bandit is unknown, but the following day Friedman recanted everything he said the day before and claimed that the whole robbery story was all a police lie and that he was forced to confess under duress. An unsuccessful attempt was made to extradite Voiler from Chicago and Morris Cohen was never found, so Friedman faced the music alone.

Mae agreed to testify against Friedman, whose trial was to begin on January 15, 1934. As the trial date approached Mae began to receive phone calls informing her that if she went on the stand she would have "plenty of trouble." "Trouble" included having acid thrown in her face. The District Attorney's office and the L.A.P.D. assigned her four guards, who both staked out her house and escorted her to and from the Paramount studio.

In the fifteen months since the robbery, Mae had gone from relatively unknown stage actress to one of the top movie stars in the country. Her successful supporting role in *Night After Night* led to a contract with Paramount Pictures, which led to two of the top five–grossing films of 1933: *She Done Him Wrong* and *I'm No Angel*. Contemplating large crowds, as there were with the Mary Pickford kidnapping trial from nearly nine years earlier, barricades were placed outside the courtroom to keep spectators at bay. Mae was to be the first witness for the prosecution but spent the first day in the judge's chambers and wasn't called. The following day she was called and, with police guard, made her way through the hundreds of people who jammed the hallway to get a look at her. In keeping with her sexy persona, the reporter from the *Los Angeles Times* noted that she "slithered" into the courtroom wearing a mink coat and a fitted dress that was black from the waist down and a deep red on top. Around her waist was a gold-link chain belt. Her hands were covered with white gloves. The ensemble was topped off with a black hat and veil. With all eyes on her, she strutted towards the witness stand with both hands placed below her hips and to the rear, smiling at everyone.

On the stand she was all business. The prosecution had her detail the robbery. In cross-examination, the defense counsel tried to get her to admit that the only reason she thought that Friedman was the man who robbed her was because the detectives told her he was the man who did it.

"You expected to meet the man that held you up when the officers telephoned you that they were bringing a suspect to your home, didn't you?" the attorney asked.

"Yes, I did expect to meet the man that held me up," Mae replied," because the officers told me that he had confessed, and then when I did meet him he confessed all over again to me."

Mae went on to say that, "Friedman told me that he held me up. He told me he was sorry that he did it, but that the thousand dollars he was to get looked like a million dollars to him."

"I told him," Mae continued, "that I was not sore at him, but that I was sore at Voiler, whom I always thought was my friend."

The one laugh that Mae did get was when the defense attorney, Mr. Clark, showed her a photograph of Friedman, naked from the waist up, supposedly showing bruises he received from the police department. When asked if she had noticed any bruises on Friedman when they met, Mae, who could make anything sound like innuendo, replied, "You know, Mr. Clark, that I have never seen anything but this defendant's face."

After Mae's appearance the trial continued for a few more weeks, and the threats against her continued as well. Guards continued to watch her house, and at four a.m. on January 24, they chased someone who tried to gain access to her apartment, but he got away. On February 3, 1934, Friedman was found guilty and was sentenced to serve from two years to life at San Quentin.

After Friedman was sent away there was still concern for Mae's safety. In early March, she started rehearsals for her next picture; the working title was *It Ain't No Sin*, but it would eventually be released as *Belle of the Nineties*. Mae received police escorts to and from the studio, and the sets were closed to anyone not involved with the movie. In addition to the police presence Mae hired a private bodyguard named Mike Mazurki. Mazurki was a wrestler who came out west from New York. A fan of both boxing and wrestling, Mae met Mazurki at a match in Pasadena and asked him to be her bodyguard. "I'll want you around all the time, see?" Mae instructed him. "Take me to the studio. Be on the set. Watch for anybody tryin' to get too close to me and ruin my face, see?" Mazurki stayed on the set and was even used as an extra, resulting in his first screen credit. (Mazurki would go on to have a successful career playing a heavy from the 1940s on.)

While work on *Belle of the Nineties* was getting started Mae was asked about her trial experience and the trouble with criminals that stars face.

"I felt somebody should put a stop to the foothold thieves and rack-eteers were attempting to gain in Hollywood," she said. "I've got to do it as a citizen; I've got to do it for society.

"They threaten us under penalty of having acid thrown in our faces, and they don't stop at acid threats either.

"It's time someone called their hand and if it has to be me, I'll do it.

"Don't think it was any pleasure session—those days in the court testifying against what investigators told me was a 'mob' that would stop at nothing. But if it means going to court as a witness to put a stop to intimidating and robbing people out here—I'll do it again."

• • •

Mae West wasn't the first member of the Hollywood community to be the victim of armed robbery. Just after midnight on April 5, 1925, debonair leading man Marc McDermott was driving in Los Angeles with a female companion named Gertrude Shirk. As McDermott neared the intersection of Bernado Street and Wilshire Boulevard, a car containing two well-dressed men forced his car to the curb. The men jumped out and ran to the actor's auto. At gunpoint, McDermott was relieved of his cash and Mrs. Shirk her jewelry. She had a hard time removing a couple of rings, and one of the robbers threatened to kill her if she didn't hurry up. She got them off in time. The bandits returned to their vehicle and made off with the $5,300 worth of loot.

Unfortunately for the Pickford-Fairbanks clan, their brushes with crime did not end with the guilty verdict of Mary's would-be kidnappers. On the evening of November 8, 1928, Mary's sister, Lottie, went out with Jack Daugherty, the husband of recently deceased actress Barbara La Marr. They spent most of the evening at a nightclub in East Los Angeles, and at around two a. m. they piled into Lottie's car and headed for home. Unfortunately they weren't all that familiar with the area and got lost. Seeing four men loitering on a corner, they pulled over and got out to ask for directions back to Hollywood. Daugherty's inquiry was met with a sap to the head. The men knocked Daugherty unconscious and robbed him; then they turned on Lottie and began to beat and kick her. The group forced Lottie back into her car and they drove off. In the car Lottie managed to remove some of her jewelry and hide it in her shoe. At some point the desperadoes pulled the car over and they attacked

Lottie again, robbing her of seventy-five dollars. They also tried getting one of her bracelets off. Since her attackers were Mexican, Lottie began repeating a short prayer she knew in Spanish and the leader of the group called off the assault. Three of the men fled the car while the other drove Lottie back to where Daugherty was still lying unconscious and left her there with the car. Lottie was able to wake Daugherty up and take him to the hospital.

Less than two years later, the first family of the cinema once again found themselves victims of bandits. Doug and Mary, together with Mary's brother Jack, went to the couple's Santa Monica beach home during the first weekend of August 1930. On Saturday evening, August 2, they went to visit a friend and returned a little after three a.m. They entered through the gate where a guard was on duty and proceeded into the house. Since there was a guard Doug felt safe leaving the rear door unlocked. He and Mary went upstairs and to their rooms; Jack was already bedded down for the evening. After a few minutes Doug went downstairs to leave a note for the servants and "As I stepped down into the light I looked right into the gun." The actor found himself staring down the barrel of an automatic pistol held by a young man whose face was covered by a handkerchief. At the doorway stood two others, their faces also obscured. Apparently the bandits were unaware of whose house they had entered because the gunman exclaimed, "Oh, it is Doug Fairbanks. Gee, Doug, I am sorry I have to do this to you, but I need the money."

"Well, so this is a hold-up?" Doug replied. He reached into his pocket and gave the gunman something in the neighborhood of thirty dollars. "I noticed that he took it even if he was sorry," Doug reported. "He acted quite decently about it—that is, if a hold-up can be decent—and turned and went quickly out the door. That was that." Doug assumed that the youthful invaders had climbed over the seawall that surrounded the house and entered through the door he left unlocked.

• • •

On the evening of October 20, 1932, Helene Costello, actress and sister in-law to John Barrymore, left her mansion, the property of which was next to oil magnate E. L. Doheny's spread, to keep an appointment with the hairdresser. Two other servants were also out, leaving only the Filipino houseboy on the premises. Moments after Ms. Costello left there was a ringing of the back door bell. The houseboy answered the door and was greeted by a man wearing dark glasses. He opened the door and the man pressed a gun into him. "Know where heaven is?" the desperado barked. The houseboy raised his hands skyward. The gunman entered followed by another man, also wearing dark glasses, carrying picture wire, a cardboard carton, and some tape; out front sat a getaway car with a driver at the wheel.

The houseboy was forced into the living room, where tape was placed over his mouth and the cardboard carton placed over his head. The men bound his wrist to his ankles with the picture wire and pushed him to the floor. Once the servant was subdued, the bandits went upstairs and ransacked Helene's bedroom and the rest of the second floor for approximately ninety minutes. While the bandits were still upstairs going about their business, the houseboy managed to wriggle himself loose and escape through the back door. He ran to the nearest neighbor, MGM film director Jack Conway, and explained to the chauffeur and housekeeper what was happening. They called the police. During that time the bandits realized that their captive had made his getaway, and they in turn were able to successfully beat it before the cops arrived.

Helene returned home to find detectives searching her bedroom for fingerprints. After going through her things, the actress stated that she was missing a triple-platinum bracelet set with a twenty-one carat diamond, three smaller diamond and platinum bracelets, a diamond and platinum necklace, and a diamond and platinum lavaliere with a pearl pendant, all of which was insured for $24,000.

• • •

Hollywood on the Spot

Actress Betty Compson had a similar experience on the evening of January 5, 1933, when the actress was spending the evening at home drinking and playing cards with her producer friend E.D. Leshin. At one point the doorbell rang. Betty answered the door to see a Western Union deliveryman. "Miss Compson?" he asked. "Yes," the actress replied, opening the door to get her message. The deliveryman immediately pulled out a gun and forced his way in. "This is a stick-up," he informed her. They returned to the living room where Leshin was waiting. "Now listen," the gunman told them, "I know my business, and if you make any squawk, I burn you both down."

The duo was forced up to Betty's bedroom, where the bandit told the actress to face the wall. Then he ordered Leshin to lie on the floor, where he bound his hands and feet with piano wire before placing tape over his mouth. Then it was Betty's turn. Before taping her mouth, however, he demanded that she tell him where she hid her jewelry, stating that he would kill her right there if she refused to do so. She told him then got taped. The robber helped himself to over $41,000 worth of jewels and left. Fifteen minutes later Betty was able to wriggle herself free and untie Leshin. They called the police, and during the initial questioning, police stated that Betty had told them that she recognized the bandit.

The following day police came back to Ms. Compson's house to get a full report and a description of the jewelry. During the interview the actress suddenly rose from the table and left the room. After a while she returned and informed the police that she didn't want to file a report after all and asked the detectives to drop the case. "I signed waivers of my insurance policies on the jewels because I feel certain they will be returned," Betty told the detectives, "My life means more than the jewels to me, and I honestly feel I am in jeopardy. I have been threatened, not only by the man who robbed me, but over the telephone."

Betty also made it a point to tell the press that the police made a mistake; according to her, she had never said that she recognized the man who robbed her. As it turned out, Betty's first version of the robbery was a lie she told out of fear for her life. "I told the police at first that the robber was in a telegraph messenger's uniform because he [the bandit] told Mr. Leshin and I just before he left: 'I'm wearing a Western Union uniform. That's what you're to tell the police, or I'll come back and get you both.'" In actuality, he was wearing a black overcoat and a slouch hat.

A police report stated that a detective, with some inside information, said that Betty received a phone call during the police interview threatening her, and that was why she refused to sign the complaint. Betty in turn said that she refused on advice from her business manager. Though she didn't confirm that she received a call during the meeting, she reiterated that her life had been threatened over the phone as well as during the robbery.

Since Ms. Compson refused to sign the complaint, authorities could not investigate the crime. A few weeks later, however, Betty paid a visit to Chief of Detectives Joe Taylor and told him that she got all her jewelry back. According to Betty, on the previous Friday night she received a letter in the mail containing a baggage-claim check with a note reading: "Take this check to the S.P. depot. Get your stones." Betty contacted her lawyer, who went and picked them up. All her jewels were there. "I was greatly surprised to get my jewelry back in this manner," she said. "I never negotiated with the bandits, nor did I pay a cent of money."

Most likely she was lying. Of course there is the chance that the bandits had a change of heart and returned her jewelry to her out of kindness, but odds are Betty paid to get her jewels back out of fear for her life. A likely scenario is that the thieves got in touch with her and stated that for a certain sum she would be able to retrieve her "stones" and the whole matter would be over. The money was delivered to a designated spot and the jewelry returned, and Betty didn't have to live in fear. The fact that she let two days pass before announcing the return of her jewelry also indicates that she may have waited because she was ordered to. According to Betty, however, she stated that the reason she waited the forty-eight hours—a perfect head start for the bandits to collect their money and leave town— was because she wanted to tell the news to Chief Taylor, who was away for the weekend, directly and to no-one else.

Hollywood on the Spot

• • •

Just a few weeks later on the evening of January 31, 1933, actress Aileen Pringle was entertaining Howard Dietz, who worked in the advertising department for Metro-Goldwyn-Mayer, and another actor named Matt Moore, at her Santa Monica beach house. After a while Moore excused himself and left. A few minutes later Pringle and Dietz were surprised by men whose faces were covered by green masks. "There were four of them altogether," Pringle later said. "They entered after having bound and gagged my servants." The servants, who lived in an apartment above the garage, were tied up first and the robbers retrieved a key to the main house and let themselves in.

"The men ordered us to keep quiet," Ms. Pringle said, "I told them there wasn't any money. I was so frightened I can scarcely remember what happened until I found myself lying on the divan tied up with ropes. Mr. Dietz was also tied and forced to lie down on another divan."

Pringle was telling the truth about having no money, and the robbers weren't interested in her jewelry. Dietz, on the other hand, was carrying a thousand dollars, which they took. The masked men then turned up the radio and ransacked the house for two hours. When they were done they helped themselves to some booze and sat around for a while. Before leaving they warned Pringle that if she went to the cops they would come back. After a bit she was able to free herself and then liberate the others. Fearing that the marauders would in fact return if she went to the police, she put off making the call to the authorities for a few hours.

• • •

Four months later, on the evening of June 1, comedian Zeppo Marx and his wife were entertaining a guest at their home when the doorbell rang. The maid was busy cooking dinner so Mrs. Marx answered the door.

At the threshold were two men with pistols pointed at her. They forced their way in and one of the gunmen had the Marxes and their guest, Allan Miller—who'd just arrived from New York—stand up and face the wall. As this was taking place the other bandit went into the kitchen and ordered the maid to turn off the stove. He cut the phone lines; then they joined the others. The maid and Mr. Miller were tied together with his belt, and her apron was used as a gag.

Mr. and Mrs. Marx were marched to their bedroom at gunpoint, where the bandits helped themselves to roughly thirty-thousand-dollars' worth of Mrs. Marx's jewelry. Taken was a platinum ring set with a twelve-carat stone, a platinum bracelet with rubies and diamonds, a pair of diamond set platinum clasps, and a platinum and diamond pin. Afterwards they forced the couple into a closet and slid a chest of drawers in front of the door.

After the bandits cleared out Zeppo managed to force the closet door open and call the police. "I'm tired," Zeppo told reporters, "tired of being robbed." When asked if he could describe the robbers he said, "No, I had a gun in the middle of my back during the entire visit." The reason that Zeppo was "tired of being robbed" was because this was the second time Mrs. Marx had lost her jewelry to thieves. The previous August 22, Zeppo went to the police after returning from a weekend at his Malibu beach house to report that someone had broken into their Hollywood abode and stole $37,500 worth of his wife's jewelry.

Mae West was a prime target for both robbers and extortionists.

He done her wrong. Mae West's "friend" Harry Voiler,
who orchestrated the armed robbery against her.

Harry Friedman, the gunman that snatched Mae West's "poke" and jewels.

Actress Betty Compson was bound, gagged, and robbed at gunpoint. She may have paid her robber to return her jewels.

A few weeks after Betty Compson was robbed, Aileen Pringle
was also bound, gagged, and robbed in her home.

Three

Shaking Down Tinseltown

More than any other crime, movie stars were plagued by extortion threats. If a certain amount of money wasn't paid by a certain date, the star could look forward to being killed, maimed or having a loved one (usually a child) kidnapped. In early December 1926 a letter arrived at the home of Mary Pickford's good pal Mabel Normand. It had been addressed to: *Lew Cody care of Mabel Normand's home, Beverly Hills*. Though Mabel and Lew were married the previous September 17, they lived separately. The letter, dated December 8, called for Mr. Cody to send three thousand dollars to a post office box in Fresno, California, or risk being killed. The letter was set aside and ignored. On December 23, another letter making the same demand and, again, threatening Cody's life if he refused was sent.

After the arrival of the second letter, Cody went to the police. Since the sender, twenty-one-year-old Vernon Shannon from Fresno, used his own name to rent the post office box, he was quickly apprehended. Once in custody he admitted to writing the letters. He also confessed to having written similar notes to Douglas Fairbanks, who never bothered to notify the police, as well as businessmen E. L. Doheny, the oil magnate whom Mary Pickford's would-be kidnappers cased for a while, and William Wrigley Jr., chewing gum tycoon.

When asked why he chose the actor, Shannon responded, "I have nothing against Cody. If I had received the money I asked for, I would have sent it back. I sent the letter to Mabel Normand's home because I read that Cody had married her and was living at her home."

• • •

For the most part, victims of professional kidnappers were, more times than not, grown men of wealthy families, but that all changed on March 1, 1932, with the kidnapping of Charles Lindbergh Jr. The nation as a whole was shocked with the story; the rich and famous were also frightened: if it could happen to a national hero like Lindy, who was safe? A little over two months later, on May 12, the body of the Lindbergh baby was found and America wept. Seventy-two hours later, while the country was still coming to terms with the murder of Lucky Lindy's child, Marlene Dietrich received a letter at her Beverly Hills home. Someone had cut out letters from magazines and had cobbled together a note:

YOUR DAUGHTER WILL BE KIDNAPPED UNLESS YOU GIVE US $10,000. HAVE THE MONEY BY MAY 16. LEAVE YOUR CAR IN FRONT OF YOUR HOME AND PUT MONEY PACKAGE ABOUT SIX INCHES FROM REAR ON REAR BUMPER. KEEP SILENT. DON'T BE CRAZY. QUICK ACTION.
      WANT ONLY $5 AND $10 BILLS. LINDBERGH BUSINESS.

The flip side read:

BETWEEN OURSELVES. BELIEVE YOU US WE WILL JUST HANG ON.

"[It was] The most afraid I have ever been in my life..." Dietrich would remember almost five decades later. The police and District Attorney were notified and Dietrich also called her Hollywood friends Josef von Sternberg and Maurice Chevalier, who rushed over with guns to aid in the protection of Marlene's daughter Maria. Though it was a nightmare for her mother ("I couldn't eat. I couldn't sleep," Marlene said of the ordeal), for the young Maria it was more of an adventure. "I felt I was in my own exciting movie and enjoyed the thrill of stardom," she remembered. "Waking up one night, I found von Sternberg on the floor by my bed, revolver ready, fast asleep. Another night, Chevalier, equally armed and ready, snoring musically." From here on out, Maria would accompany her mother to the movie studio every day.

Police directed Dietrich to ignore the letter while they investigated and the actress complied. While this was happening, the wife of a German linen importer named Egon Muller received a note demanding $500 under the threat of kidnapping her son. Over the course of the next two weeks Marlene received a couple more letters. One on May 25 stated,

MAMA, LISTEN DON'T BE A FOOL. OTHERS PAID ALL AND SO WILL YOU.

On May 30, another letter arrived:

YOU CAN DECIDE FOR YOURSELF. YOUR MONEY OR DEATH NOTICE. WHAT ABOUT IT? LINDBERGH BUSINESS!

As this was taking place the aforementioned Mrs. Muller received instructions to leave five hundred dollars under a designated palm tree. Instead of the whole ransom Mrs. Muller was told by police to leave only seventeen dollars. A few days later Dietrich received yet another note from the kidnappers. This one was a bit perplexing as it commanded that she pay "...

the $483 you forgot to leave!" Mrs. Muller, to her surprise, also received an equally strange message from her son's would be kidnappers.

> YOU MARLENE DIETRICH, IF YOU WANT TO SAVE MARIA TO BE A SCREEN STAR, PAY AND IF YOU DON'T SHE'LL BE BUT A LOVING MEMORY TO YOU. DON'T DARE TO CALL DETECTIVES AGAIN. KEEP THIS TO YOURSELF. SAY, WHAT'S THE BIG IDEA! ATTENTION! IS THE FUTURE OF YOUR GIRL WORTH IT? WAIT FOR NEW INFORMATION. $10,000 OR PAY HEAVILY LATER ON. YOU'LL BE SORRY. DON'T CALL THE POLICE OR DETECTIVES AGAIN.

The police, who were skeptical about the letters in the first place, were now convinced that they were dealing with some knuckle-headed amateurs. The letters were printed in the newspapers and that put an end to the whole ordeal. No other ransom letters arrived.

Because of her mother's fear for her safety, Maria would never see the inside of a public school; instead, she would be tutored at home. Two armed bodyguards took shifts guarding the family. Home security took a priority; bars were placed on the windows and an alarm system was installed. Family outings were a thing of the past. Though the Dietrich extortion case was an obvious attempt by bunglers looking to cash in on the fear induced by the Lindbergh tragedy, it had a most sobering effect on Dietrich, robbed her of any sense of freedom she may have had, and tainted her experience in California. "The worst thing that came of it," Dietrich would say, "was I was permanently more frightened for Maria in Hollywood, and I never escaped that, so the letter had its effect. I couldn't smell the orange blossoms."

Hollywood did not sleep any sounder knowing that Marlene Dietrich's tormentors were buffoons, nor were extortionists deterred from trying to shake down the stars by the bungled job. The threats kept coming: Norma Shearer and Irving Thalberg received threats against their son Irving Jr., so around-the-clock guards were hired and the toddler's nurse, who stayed with him during waking hours, slept in an adjoining room. Ann Harding also employed two armed guards to guarantee around-the-clock protection for her daughter Jane Bannister. There was always a guard at home and one to escort Jane to school or wherever else she went. Having been raised on an army base where there were always armed sentries, Ann didn't feel that having two armed men around the house would be a big deal for her daughter. For additional security, she refused to allow her daughter to be photographed with her for any sort of publicity.

To protect his three children, Harold Lloyd turned his estate into an impenetrable fortress complete with armed guards. A wall was built around his Beverly Hills estate and one of the guards pulled duty at the front gate, stopping every vehicle to inquire the reason for their visit. Other guards patrolled the estate around the clock. Armed guards also shadowed the children wherever they went. As an extra precaution, bars were placed on the kids' bedroom and nursery windows.

That fall, actor Richard Arlen went to the police and newspapers saying that he believed that he was the target of kidnappers. In mid-October he stated that, "I first felt that I was being followed about a month ago when I left the Universal studios after midnight. The auto stayed behind me almost to my door, but I forgot the matter." The "matter" came back to him shortly after nine p.m. on October 12, when he pulled out of the Paramount lot in his sixteen-cylinder yellow Phaeton. "Headlights from the trailing car flashed in the rearview mirror," he said, "and I determined to settle definitely a suspicion that had been in my mind for more than four weeks." The actor went on to say that, "As we pulled away from the studio I took side streets and on two occasions circled blocks, only to have my trailers keep me within sight of their headlights. As I raced through the Cahuenga Pass, the dark-colored roadster with its two men kept up the same speed. Before I reached my home, I doubled back in an attempt to get a look at their faces, but they wore their hats well over their eyes." After parking in his garage he went into the house and informed his wife, actress Jobyna Ralston, of the situation; together, they went to the window and, "we watched the same car as it drove around our home two or three times. Finally they left." After reporting the incident the police parked a car outside Arlen's home, located at 10025 Toluca Lake Avenue. This seemed to scare the would-be kidnappers away, as he wasn't bothered again.

Despite all the press given to how the stars were protecting themselves and guarding their homes, the threats still came. One of those who found his peace shattered was Bing Crosby, who, in the spring of 1934, received a letter threatening his son Gary if he didn't pay up. Crosby immediately contacted the authorities. He also had himself and his brother, Everett, sworn in as deputy sheriffs so that they could carry guns. Unlike a lot of the stars, who chose not to discuss the extortion threats that they faced, Crosby had no problem talking about it.

"Well, it strikes you numb with terror at first." Bing said of receiving a threatening letter. "Life simply changed completely overnight for my wife and myself, and our families. It is as if an ice pail had been thrown over all of us."

Bing also stated that, times being what they were with the Depression and all, he could understand why somebody might try shaking down movie stars but they, the stars, actually made poor targets because they weren't as rich as everyone thought. "With the disturbed economic conditions in the country, men out of work, families losing their homes, and children not getting enough to eat, in many, many instances—it's understandable why embitterment fills the hearts of persons who read about the other fellow making a fabulous fortune, when they have nothing themselves. I'd feel that way myself if the conditions were reversed.

"But if the unvarnished truth were told about Hollywood incomes— if the correct figures, and not the phony and highly colored ones, were actually stated after deducting income taxes, and commissions, and living expenses necessary for the peculiar position in which our work places us—then it would be discovered that most of us are far from being rich." He went on to state that he would consider himself lucky if he could save 15 to 20 percent of his annual salary. Lest anyone get the idea that he was a rich man crying poor, he also brought up the fact that a star's light could dim at any time, or as Bing put it, that a performer could "take a box office toboggan", and the money spigot could be turned off.

When asked if he was uncomfortable with going public with his extortion troubles he responded with, "I should say not. I think it's a mistake not to let the public know what's happening. Ann Harding, Marlene Dietrich, Mae West, and a number of other film stars have made known threats against their homes and lives, and I think they have been wise in so doing.

"A large percentage of Hollywood folks who have received kidnapping and extortion threats have adopted the attitude of silence. I don't think that silence is going to help stamp out these frightful crimes. I think those of us who have had the bad luck to be put on the spot should yell our troubles to the police and public. If we all pull together to wipe out crime, we will get someplace." Like most the other threats against the stars, the only beneficiary of the Crosby scare was the security industry. Crosby hired armed guards for his family as well as himself, and had the most up-to-date alarm system installed at his house.

• • •

On February 25, 1935 a letter arrived at the Hal Roach studios in Culver City, California, addressed to film comedienne Thelma Todd. The letter had been sent from Long Island City, New York, and read:

Pay $10,000 to Abe Lyman in New York by March 5 and live if not our San Francisco boys will lay you out. This is no joke

For a signature the writer drew a playing card depicting the ace of hearts.

Abe Lyman was a popular bandleader who Thelma had an affair with in the early 1930s; though they planned to wed, the couple broke off the engagement in 1931. Assuming that the letter was one of myriad of extortion notes arriving in Hollywood fan mail everyday, nothing was done. On March 4, another letter arrived stating:

> Don't forget the $10,000 for our San Francisco boys and pay to Abe Lyman.

This, too, was signed by "the ace of hearts."

After the arrival of the second letter, with March 5 closing in, the studio decided to go public with the extortion notes. Once the press printed the letters, the Los Angeles office of the FBI and the local police became involved. In New York G-Men visited Abe Lyman, who shrugged the whole thing off saying that it was probably a prank. Thelma took it more seriously. She hired a bodyguard of three men for protection while Hollywood and Santa Monica police routinely patrolled her home and neighborhood.

Throughout the spring and summer of 1935 "Ace" continued to send letters to Miss Todd while the FBI vainly tried to capture him. To ensure the actress's safety, G-Men would follow her to and from the studio. On March 27, another curt note was received.

> "Hurry up with the $10,000"

was all it said; this too was signed with an "Ace." The only difference with this letter was that it was mailed from Grand Central station in Manhattan as opposed to Queens. Throughout the spring and into summer "Ace" mailed a number of letters from either Long Island City or Grand Central station demanding the ten thousand. FBI men analyzed each letter in hopes of finding a clue, but none were forthcoming. They also had men stake out mailboxes in each vicinity in a futile hope of breaking the case.

On July 15, a letter was mailed from City Hall in Manhattan and was addressed to the bandleader Abe Lyman. It was an extortion letter, and though he assumed it was a prank, he turned it over to the FBI. The handwriting wasn't exactly the same and, unlike the Todd letters, this one was signed by a Tad Dorgan or Tad Dugan; the handwriting was sloppy, so authorities weren't sure of the name. After FBI handwriting specialist studied the note they determined that it was written by the same man who had penned the Todd extortion letters, only he was trying to disguise his handwriting.

At the time he received the letter Lyman was booked at a Manhattan restaurant and the G-Men began an investigation of the employees. There was one who lived in Long Island City, so they staked out his apartment house at 31-18 Newton Avenue. They watched him for a week and were able to get a sample of his handwriting. It didn't match any of the extortion notes. The FBI wasn't willing to give up on the address, so they went to the renting agent and asked to see the signatures on the leases to compare with the extortion letters. The only problem with this method was that not everyone living in the building signed the lease. Most times only the husband signed for the family and there were multiple family members living under one lease. However they did come across one signature that resembled the handwriting of the extortionist: it was the building superintendent, Harry Schimanski.

Since the FBI couldn't very well pin the crime on Schimanksi without evidence to back them up, they began to shadow the super. He was followed everywhere and his mail was constantly monitored, but no evidence showed up. Frustrated, the G-Men hit upon a new idea. They would send a telegram addressed to "Tad Dorgan" to Schimanski's apartment. If the super accepted the telegram then that meant he was guilty; if he didn't accept it, he would be innocent.

With a number of FBI agents hiding near the apartment, a messenger with the telegram rang Schimanski's bell. What happened next is up for debate. According to the FBI, Schimanksi accepted the telegram but then noticed an agent in the street and handed it back to the messenger. Schimanksi claimed that he didn't accept it. The messenger said he didn't remember what happened. Regardless, the superintendent was taken into custody. After being questioned at the FBI headquarters, Schimanski was officially arrested on August 18. On September 2, Schimanski was indicted in Federal Court for attempted extortion. His trial was set for November 10. Believing in Schimanski's innocence, the owner of the apartment building where Schimanski lived and worked posted his bail.

Towards the end of August, Thelma was interviewed at her Santa Monica restaurant in regards to the arrest of Schimanski. The actress stated that since the arrest, no more extortion letters had arrived. She went on to say, "I haven't been advised lately what has been done toward disposing of the man's arrest. I expect more word from government officials later. The arrest of the suspect does give me the satisfaction of clearing implications that this letter-writing business was a publicity stunt.

"So far as I am concerned," Ms. Todd continued, "there doesn't have to be a prosecution but I am ready to follow any advice investigators may give. It would be extremely difficult for me to go to New York to attend a trial." Thelma also stated that thanks to the FBI she could once again go about freely without worrying about her safety.

For a few days it appeared to everyone that the case was closed until September 4, when a postcard arrived at the offices of the Long Island *Daily Star* newspaper. It was addressed to the editor and read:

Here is the prove[sic] that man held in Todd case is innocent.
"Pay $10,000 to Abe Lyman in New York an live if not our San Francisco boys lay you out. This is no joke."

It was signed with the familiar "ace" of hearts. The editor turned the card over to reporter Andrew Viglietta. Viglietta had been following the case since the beginning when he was working in Hollywood. He had previously interviewed Schimanski and felt he was innocent.

Viglietta took the postcard to the FBI headquarters in Manhattan, where it was procured and sent to Washington for analysis. The reporter was told that if any more cards, or better yet phone calls, were received by "Ace," to let them know. About three weeks later on September 29, the editor of the *Daily Star* received a phone call. The caller reminded the editor about the postcard he received earlier that month. The caller asked that the card be turned over to the FBI and hung up.

Viglietta went to the FBI offices with the news of the phone call. The G-Men weren't concerned. Word had been received from the labs in Washington, D.C.—the handwriting specialist had concluded that the postcard received by the newspaper had been written by Schimanski, who was out on bail.

October came and went without any new word about the case, but on the morning of November 3, as Schimanski's trial date drew near, the editor at the *Daily Star* received another call.

"Are you going to help me or not?" the caller pleaded, "This is the man who wrote the extortion notes to Thelma Todd. Schimanski is innocent. I can't give myself up to the police. But you can help me if you want to. Will you?"

In an attempt to keep the caller on the line long enough to trace the call, the editor said he couldn't hear him and asked him to repeat what he had just said. The caller complied.

"What is your name?" asked the editor.

"Richard Harding," the caller answered after a brief hesitation. "Please put a piece in your paper that Schimanski is innocent. He had nothing to do with the case. I did it to give Thelma Todd publicity."

"Are you the man who sent the postal card to *The Star*?" asked the editor.

"Yes, on September third," replied the caller.

"Do you know Schimanski?" asked the editor.

"Sure I know Schimanksi…" the caller started then stopped. After a few moments he began again,

"Not personally, you know. I only know what I read about him. But I must go to work now. Goodbye."

Though they were unsuccessful in tracing the call, the editor typed up the conversation and Viglietta ran it over to the FBI who, once again, weren't impressed. In their view, if Schimanski had written the postcard from September 3, as their labs had stated, then he was probably making the phone calls too. Viglietta returned to *The Star* offices where he was ordered to stand by in case Richard Harding called back. At one p.m. the call came through. The reporter gave his name as Charles Brown and the caller went on to say that, "I am the man who sent those letters to Miss Todd. Do you know about that? Honest, I didn't mean any harm. I love the girl. I wanted her to get publicity out of it. I want to free this man Schimanski who is charged with the crime." Viglietta said that he believed him and thought that Schimanski was innocent as well. The caller then gushed over the actress some more. "Honest, I'm in love with the girl. I tell you I'm in love with her and I had to do something to let her know that I am her admirer. Why, I spent my last ten bucks to wire her orchids for her birthday. So you see I'd rather starve if I could only give her something."

Viglietta concurred that Ms. Todd was indeed beautiful and mentioned that he had met her when he was working in Hollywood and even got to see her do some filming. Harding was mesmerized by this and kept asking him questions about Tinseltown. Meanwhile the newspaper was able to call the FBI office and have them patched into the call so they could listen. After a bit Harding began to get suspicious. "I wonder whether I can trust you," he said. "I don't want to be arrested. It'll be too bad for you if I am."

Viglietta played along. "I know it will be too bad for me," he answered, "But I'm no fool. I don't want to be bumped off. I'm not going to tell the cops. All I want is a story. I believe you. I want you to trust me just as I am trusting you." After thinking it over, Harding responded, "I think you're all right. I want you to put a piece in the paper about Schimanski. Tell them I did it. My name is Richard Harding and I want it put in the paper today." With that, the caller hung up.

The call was traced to a drugstore phone booth on John Street in lower Manhattan. By the time agents got there numerous other people had used it, so dusting for fingerprints was useless. The only information of any value was that a clerk for the store said he remembered a tall, skinny guy with a dark complexion who was on the phone for a long time.

Later that afternoon the FBI met with Viglietta. The G-Men felt that "Richard Harding" was in fact Schimanski trying to exonerate himself.

Viglietta said that he believed that the caller was someone else entirely. The FBI agents then told the reporter to go and interview Schimanski again and pay attention to his voice. Viglietta went to the Astoria address and spoke with the superintendent about the upcoming trial. He noted that both the caller and this man had remarkably similar voices.

The following day there was no piece about Schimanski being innocent. At about 3:00 p.m. on the afternoon of November 5, "Richard Harding" called *The Star*. He wanted to know why the piece wasn't in the paper. Viglietta told him that the editor refused and only wanted to print a feature story. "He wants me to get the human interest angle," Viglietta lied. The reporter also stated that the only way they could continue is if they met face to face. At first "Harding" declined but Viglietta managed to gain his confidence by saying, "All I want is a story. I saw Schimanski last night and I know that he is entirely innocent. I don't want to put anybody in jail. But I want to free an innocent man and I want a good story for my newspaper." After some more back and forth, the caller agreed to meet with the reporter at a newsstand that specialized in out-of-town newspapers behind the old Times Building in Times Square. This perplexed the reporter, "Aren't there too many people there?" he asked, "We ought to be alone. I don't want anyone to know about this."

"I don't want anyone to know about it either," the caller replied. "But no one will bother us there. I go there every day to buy out-of-town newspapers from Hollywood, so I can read news about Thelma Todd." The two men agreed to meet that afternoon at 4:00 p.m. Viglietta jumped into a cab and headed into Manhattan. He stopped at the FBI office, which was a few avenues over from the rendezvous spot. Three agents joined him and they made their way to Times Square. It was determined that when Viglietta was certain that he was talking with "Richard Harding" he would tip his hat and the agents would close in. As they approached the newsstand the agents broke off and took up positions nearby. The reporter stood at the newsstand reading a copy of *The Star*. Looking up he saw a tall, skinny man in shabby clothes standing at the entrance to the subway. Viglietta walked up to him and the man took the newspaper from him and read the title.

With paper in hand, his eyes darted about to make sure there was nobody else around. Then he asked, "Your name is Brown?"

"Yes," the reporter answered. "And you are Richard Harding?"

"Yes, I am Dick Harding. Are you alone?"

The reporter assured Harding that they were alone. The tall, skinny man suggested that they get a bite to eat and that he would give him the whole story. The two men began to walk and then Viglietta raised his hat. "Harding" made a move to run, but the agents were on him before he had a chance to get away.

"You, I'll get you for this!" he screamed at the reporter.

"Richard Harding" turned out to be Edward Schiffert, a 26-year-old man who lived with his parents in the same building as Harry Schimanski. Schiffert admitted to writing all the letters and after some questioning he was sent to Bellevue Hospital, where he was declared insane. His parents refused to believe that he was the culprit. They described him as "mentally unsound" but not insane. "He got the idea, somehow, that Schimanski was innocent," Schiffert's mother said, "and he used to brood over it. He said he was going to protect Schimanski. We thought it was just another one of his ideas and didn't pay any attention." Authorities saw it differently, however. On November 14, Schimanski was exonerated of all charges and on December 3, Schiffert was sent to the mental institution on New York City's Ward's Island.

• • •

As the Thelma Todd case was winding down, Mae West once again found herself dealing with those who would do her harm. On September 2, 1935, a postman showed up at her apartment with a letter sent "special delivery." Mae opened it and found a note. Handwritten in pencil, it read:

Acid is a horrible deed to throw in one's face so beautiful in the heights of her career for the small sum of one thousand dollars.

We could have did it many times already but we want to see what you would say first. We had your chauffeur's automatic last Friday but put it back. Ask him if he left it in the car and then come back for it an hour later.

You can tell the police if you wish. But then you will be sure to get acid and a little lye in the eyes as good measure. We want one thousand dollars in 5s, 10s and 20s, unmarked or copied. If so you shall never be afraid again of this threat as we keep our promise. We told you two yrs. ago you would get it some time so kick in if you don't want to lose, lose your career and beauty. We are going to give you a little facts.

On the set – or fight or home or riding or parties or studio. We see you every day. If you care to put ad in morning paper, person ad, by Tuesday Night 'I will, M. W.' and we will get touch with you. Tell timoney we know Him personally, bye,

ACID BURNS

Mae took the letter to the District Attorney's office. Extortion notes were nothing new to movie stars but whereas most of the "facts" that the writer(s) of Mae's letter described could have been gathered by anyone—of course she went to the studio, to parties, and was known to attend the fights on a regular basis—there was one passage that proved that the extortionist were indeed shadowing her, the bit about Mae's chauffeur/bodyguard, Albert "Chalky" Wright, leaving his gun in the car then coming back for it an hour later. This incident actually happened so Mae knew she was dealing with something serious.

Investigators for the District Attorney told Mae to go ahead and put the ad in the paper. On September 6, another letter arrived at her apartment, special delivery.

Seen your ad. If this is a police trap you will regret it. You ans. in personal by Saturday morning. Give telephone number. We are not fools. We don't intend to take a rap for you. We have you cased.

We seen police go in there Mon. eve. Call them off or else. We don't joke. Answer same way.

ACID BURNS

Nothing was done about the second letter. A week later on September 13, Mae's bell rang; it was another letter via special delivery.

We told you before $1000 or you have your face lifted. Sunday by 8 o'clock or by two we will get your face at Western and Sunset, you personally.

ACID BURNS

Again no action was taken, resulting in a fourth letter which was delivered on September 30.

Acid is a holely job. It never heals. We have an air gun which will shoot 100 yards and it has a perfect sight. We know we would be caught if we walk up to you an throw it in your face so we are playing it safe. We want $1000 by Tuesday nite at 12 o'clock. There is a tin can in front of studio on Sunset Blvd. There a passage there. It's inside the concrete wall. Next to the hydrant tie a white handkerchief on faucet so we know it there. Cross us an lose a million. We will send a decoy for it.
　　"Love to Timothy and brother West
　　"Acid Burns"

When writing "Timothy," the extortionist most likely meant "Timoney," Mae's manager; brother West would have been Mae's sibling, John West. A plan was put into effect where the ransom would be delivered and agents would be on hand to arrest the extortionist when they picked up the money. To avoid any possible danger coming to Mae, an investigator for the District Attorney named Harry Dean donned a platinum wig, makeup, and a woman's hat and coat. Posing as Mae, Dean sat in the back of the car while Chalky drove to the designated spot and delivered the package. Hidden all around the spot were numerous armed detectives waiting to pounce. The extortionist however, sensing a setup, didn't make a move. Instead, another letter was sent to Mae on October 2.

We seen your sign. It looked like a trap. You put the money next to the fire plug over the wall in the bushes tonite and leave it there in a tin can. A small can of your own. If anyone stops the man who comes for it this town will be too hot to hold you as he will not know who we are and we don't joke. We seen timothy without you last nite at the fights. You sent one guy up the rever [sic] for publicity so don't try it again.
"Acid Burns"

Once again, Dean dressed as Mae and was driven out by Chalky to drop off the money. The extortionist saw through the plot and didn't go for the bait. Instead a sixth and final letter was received on Monday October 7.

Acid is a horrible thing to throw in one's face so beautiful in the heights of her career. You can lose a $1000 or 1,000,000. We are determined to get it. We want that money no later than nine o'clock Monday night in the last tree palm tree. If the extortion squad is there we will by our o[a]th get you and spoil your face for all time. You know where the last three[tree] is by the gate on the corner. Stick it in the tree by the palms and don't try to stop who gets it. Tie a handkerchief on the wall there opposite the tree. If you fail to meet our demands we will shoot a air gun at you within ten da's and we are good shots. If one of the three of us is caught by the cop you get one in the head. Put it there a 7 o'clock sharp personally. We will be watching. Tell Timothy Hello. Will see him Tuesday.
"Bye"

"ACID BURNS"

"Put in a wrapper 5-10-20 no later at seven sharp. Use your own car. A dummy will get you nowhere."

This time it was decided that Mae would deliver the package herself. This time investigator Dean, sans Mae West drag, and another agent crouched on the floor of Mae's car while Chalky drove to the drop-off. In parked cars, doorways, and hidden behind nearby buildings were a number of officers armed with shotguns and machine guns. At the designated time Mae's limousine pulled up. The actress alighted from her car and stashed the package in the palm tree as dictated. She climbed back into the car and Chalky took her home. Twenty-five minutes later a man sauntered up and grabbed the package. Detectives quickly fell on him and he was taken into custody.

Mae was asked if she was scared when she dropped off the package. "Of course I was scared," she said as if delivering a line in a film. "What do you think I am an icicle?" The arrested man was a 38-year-old Greek immigrant named George Janios who worked as a busboy at the Warner Brothers' commissary. He claimed that he had been sitting in a coffee shop when he saw a large car pull up across the street and saw a woman plant a package in the tree. Curious, he went out and grabbed it. Authorities weren't inclined to believe him since he waited nearly half an hour to retrieve the package, but after holding him for twenty-four hours they decided he was telling the truth and let him go. Though the District Attorney's office failed in getting the extortionists, the arrest of Janios apparently convinced the hoodlums that they wouldn't be successful because Mae didn't receive another letter from them.

• • •

Adult stars weren't the only targets of extortionists. Child stars also received their fair share of threats. In the mid-1930s threatening letters were sent to both Jane Withers and Freddie Bartholomew, which resulted in body guards for each, but it was Shirley Temple, the top-drawing star from 1935 to 1938, who helped keep the G-Men busy in the summer of 1936.

On May 8, Sterling Powell, a sixteen-year-old schoolboy from Grant, Nebraska, went to the movies. The picture that day was a crime film that revolved around extortion. Afterwards, Powell got the idea that he might want to try shaking down a star. He decided on Shirley Temple and wrote a letter to the starlet's father, George, care of Twentieth Century Fox. The letter was short and to the point:

> "Unless $25,000 is dropped from an airplane near Grant, Neb., on May 15, the life of Shirley Temple will be endangered."

Though his conscience told him not to, Powell dropped the letter in the mail. Over the next few weeks he was nervous about the possible outcome of his actions. According to George Temple, he received on average about fifty letters a month that could have been considered threats. Why Powell's letter received more attention than others in unknown; perhaps it was because it wasn't opened until May 18, three days after the payoff demand, but the mail readers at Fox decided to forward it to the FBI instead of simply tossing it, and G-Men went to work tracing the letter.

It took most of the summer, but investigators were able to track the paper Powell used to the manufacture and from there to sales in the town of Grant and nearby Madrid. How they narrowed it down to Powell was never divulged. On July 29, with thoughts of the letter well behind him, Powell was out working the farm with his parents when the sheriff showed up. After a few questions Sterling admitted to writing the letter and was taken away.

About a week after Powell was arrested, another letter arrived at Twentieth Century Fox. This one, though addressed to Mrs. Shirley Temple, was meant for Shirley's mother, Gertrude. Like the previous letter it demanded $25,000 stating, "Get the money if you want to keep Shirley." The FBI received another call from the movie studio. The writer of this note was also a sixteen-year-old boy, but whereas Sterling Powell had enough imagination to attempt avoiding capture by having his ransom dropped by a plane, the writer of the second note, one Frank Stephens, wanted it delivered to the grocery store where he worked part time in Atlanta, Georgia. Not that it helped, but Stephens did have the foresight to at least use the alias Curtis Palmer. Local G-Men stopped into the store and questioned the owner, who said he'd never heard of this Palmer person. During the investigation detectives questioned Stephens and before long he found himself confessing.

• • •

In the mailroom of RKO Studios one of the clerks came across a letter addressed to Virginia Rogers. It was postmarked November 26, 1936, and he assumed that the writer was more than an average fan since devotees of this star usually simply addressed their letters to Ginger Rogers. The clerk opened it and read:

> Virginia Rogers - I want $5000 or else you and your mother will be filled so full of holes you will be like a sieve. I have been watching you and your mother all the time. Any attempt to notify police and we will kill your mother and if you don't believe it, make one slip and we will get her and you both.
>
> I want bills in 100, 50 and 20 denominations. You will proceed to Long Beach. Wednesday, Dec. 9. You will be followed by two of my men. You will wrap the money in paper and leave it at the Anchorage Café or beer parlor at 11 P.M. You will make an attempt to disguise yourself so you will not be known.
>
> Make no slip, OR ELSE –

The clerk ran the letter over to his superiors and they in turn contacted the FBI. Soon after, Ginger Rogers received a call at home from a G-Man apprising her of the situation. The agent told her that she should go about her business and that they would be keeping an eye on her. Rogers continued rehearsing with Fred Astaire for their upcoming film *Shall We Dance*, and when she left the studio, a car filled with agents would pull out and follow her home. If she went out for dinner, agents would be seated nearby. Two days later another letter arrived in the RKO mailroom. At the top, written in red pencil was the word "Warning" in capital letters. The body of the text, written in normal pencil, read:

> Just to remind you that you are being watched, and you are acting suspicious. If you get too suspicious you will be taken care of. The $5,000 will be in unmarked bills. You change the date of delivery from Dec. 9 to Dec. 4, Friday at 11 P.M.
>
> The Anchorage Café is down past the navy landing and you had better not forget. You had better not be recognized and better not be followed by the cops.

It was signed again with the red pencil "Last warning."

Though Rogers wanted to take part in the operation that would capture her tormentor by personally delivering the package to the Anchorage Café, the G-Men refused. So on the evening of December 4, she went to the movies while the FBI agents went to Long Beach.

The following morning Rogers and her mother learned, along with everyone else, that the perpetrator had been caught when J. Edgar Hoover made an announcement from Washington, D.C. The writer of the letters turned out to be a twenty-year-old sailor assigned to the aircraft carrier *Lexington* named James Hall. The FBI agents refused to give all the details of the arrest, but Hall was picked up after loitering about the Anchorage Café for an hour or so.

Once in custody, Hall confessed to the plot. He said that Rogers was his favorite actress and that he fell in love with her after seeing *Follow the Fleet*. As for the extortion attempt, "I read a lot about people getting money that way and I thought I'd try it," he said. Hall was quickly arraigned and held under $25,000 bail. When informed that he was facing a serious charge and needed a lawyer he replied, "I don't want an attorney. I got caught and I want to take my medicine."

When questioned about the case Rogers said, "I am taken by surprise, spellbound. I don't know what to do or say. The *Lexington* is one of my favorite boats, too. I'm glad they caught him, but I am sorry he was such a young man. I feel more at ease now with this out of the way." She also mentioned that, "I didn't know about the letters until the Federal men phoned me. That made it rather frightening, to be phoned by G-Men."

Rogers's mother, Lela, was also affected by the extortionist's age. "When threatening letters are received one thinks of great, bearded men and then when one finds it is some child one just goes to pieces." This wasn't the first time Ginger Rogers received threatening letters. Another came to the studio prior to Hall's but it was ignored. "Notes of this type come through and the players never see them," her mother stated. "The studio fan mail departments get them first and the first thing anybody knows there is a bodyguard assigned to you. That's what happened to us."

Fifty-five years later Ginger discussed the extortion case in her autobiography but over the course of nearly six decades some of the details were misremembered. For instance she states that the sailor was on the *USS Texas* and not the *Lexington* and that the payoff was to take place in San Pedro, not Long Beach. She also stated that the extortion letter was brought to her and that she took it to the FBI against the studio's wishes. Another difference was that she wrote that she was actually on the premises of the café during the arrest of Hall. None of which is backed up by contemporary reports.

• • •

Though kidnapping and extortion threats against the stars didn't exactly end with the Depression, there were far fewer publicized attempts, and of those that did make the press, most were of the juvenile sort that plagued Shirley Temple five years before.

One such attempt came on March 7, 1940, when the Culver City police received a phone call.

"Do you know Judy Garland?" a male caller asked.

"Yes," the officer taking the call replied.

"Well, she's going to be kidnapped tonight," the caller stated before hanging up. Three police cars were immediately sent to patrol the Bel-Air neighborhood where Judy lived, while two detectives went to her house at 1231 Stone Canyon Road to inform the family of the threat. They found Judy and her sister Virginia entertaining half a dozen friends. Her mom and step-dad were out. The detectives informed Judy of the call and that they would be sticking around to protect her. "I've never been threatened before," she told them, "I'm sure everything will be all right—but make yourselves at home." Somewhere along the line the press caught wind of the situation and a photographer got himself into the house where he photographed Judy serving the detectives refreshments. She also continued her small party with her friends until her mother returned home. Meanwhile the call was traced to a hotel lobby in Santa Monica. Detectives got a description of the caller from a bellboy and managed to pick up nineteen-year-old Robert Wilson as he exited a nearby theater. Wilson told police that he and an accomplice named Foster had watched Judy's house for two nights and knew that her servants would be off Thursday night. The duo planned to break into her house at midnight and make off with the young actress, taking her to the mountains and holding her for ransom. Wilson then got cold feet and placed the call to the police.

As police questioned Wilson his responses began to contradict other answers and after a while he admitted that there was no "Foster" and there never was a plot to kidnap Judy. He simply said that the whole thing was a ruse because "I just wanted to meet her." He was turned over for psychiatric examination. "I guess I fell in love with Judy by seeing her in pictures." Wilson stated. "Every time she wiggles that cute little pug nose of hers, I fall more in love with her. She is my dream girl."

Though Judy wasn't concerned her mother, Ethel Gumm Gilmore, was. She mentioned to police that a young man had called the house numerous times asking for Judy. She went on to say that another young man had followed her to the studio a couple of times and stopped her to take a picture. "I love Judy Garland" had also been scribbled on their mailbox in red crayon. Whether any of these acts was attributed to Wilson is unknown.

• • •

A few weeks before Christmas 1940, a letter for Betty Grable arrived in the RKO Studios mailroom. Postmarked December 6 and mailed from Washington, Pennsylvania, the letter informed the actress that:

"You have been selected by me, the Yellow Hornet, to pay the sum of $2000. The amount will be sent by special delivery, any way you prefer, by December 25. Christmas day, or you will thus suffer the result.

"This is not a joke, but strictly business. If you, however, don't send the money…, I will personally com out an get you."

The extortion note was signed "Betty Westlake, alias the Yellow Hornet."

RKO staff turned the letter over to the FBI, and agents were dispatched to Washington, Pennsylvania. They paid a visit to the address given in the extortion letter and found that a family named Westlake actually lived there, although there was no "Betty" in the family. The homeowner's young daughter, however, told the agents that she also received a threatening letter, as did fourteen other people in the township of Washington, informing them that they had been chosen to join the "Yellow Hornets Club." Each letter had a specific instruction for the recipient to follow under threat of harm if they should fail. G-Men were able to trace the letters to an eighteen-year-old boy named James Willard

Porter who was quickly arrested. A clergyman speaking on behalf of the family said, "Illness compelled James to leave high school two years ago. He has been very sick, complaining of a severe pain in the head. He spent some time in a tuberculosis sanitarium. He is very timid and very nice, coming from a splendid family. This incident was evidently just a boyish prank and is a great shock to everybody." A Federal judge agreed; after Porter pleaded guilty he was sentenced to eighteen months, but the judge immediately suspended the sentence and the "Yellow Hornet" was released.

Hardly a month went by before another letter arrived from Pennsylvania on January 24, 1941. This one demanded that Grable mail $8,500 to a Philadelphia address in care of General Delivery. To not send it would result in physical harm. The local FBI office was given charge of the matter and in short order had arrested twenty-four-year-old ex-convict James Thomson who was now working as a singing waiter. On February 28, he pleaded guilty and was sentenced to one year and one day.

On February 6, 1943, Grable received yet another letter informing her that if she didn't place $25,000 in uncut diamonds into two separate envelopes and send them to a hotel in downtown Hollywood she would be killed. The note was signed "the Leopard." The letter was turned over to the FBI who mailed two dummy letters to the address and then had undercover agents stake out the hotel waiting to nab the extortionist, but he never showed up.

On March 9, another letter arrived from "the Leopard" directing Grable to drive along Gower Street on March 19, and, when she saw a man "leaning against a wall" between Melrose Avenue and Sunset Boulevard, she was to throw a package containing five thousand dollars from the car and continue driving. Once again, death would be the penalty if she failed to do so. This letter, too, was turned over to Federal agents. At the designated time a female agent, made up to look like Ms. Grable, drove into position. Other cars traveling up and down the street contained G-Men, while other agents were on hand looking like average civilians. The Grable impostor threw the money from the car as directed and a young man ran up and grabbed it. Once it was in his possession he began to run but was apprehended within seconds.

"The Leopard" turned out to be an eighteen-year-old high school student named Russell Alexanderson. He grew up in Omaha, Nebraska, but moved out west because his mother got a job in an aircraft plant while his dad was off in the army. Once in custody Russell assured authorities he had no intention of actually killing Grable. "I wanted the money only to enable me to meet movie stars," he said during his arraignment, "I had no opportunity to see them because I had to account to my mother for every dime I spent."

Mae West read the story the following day in the newspapers and a light bulb went off in her head. She retrieved a threatening letter she'd received about a month before demanding that she, "under threat of your life or great bodily harm" deliver a package containing $100,000 to 6233 Hollywood Boulevard on February 6. It was signed "The Leopard." She turned it over to the authorities. On March 29, Russell plead guilty to writing both letters, stating that he only wanted to meet a movie star face to face. He was found guilty, but the judge suspended the sentence and he was released on five years' probation.

Around the middle of May, Grable received another letter. This one instructed her to bring five hundred dollars to the office of the Federal Probation Service at a designated time on May 18. Once again G-Men showed up in Grable's stead and once again Russell Alexanderson was taken into custody.

"If I could have seen her once there would have been no other crime," Russell said. "I hoped she would appear in answer to my letter, that's all." The troubled teenager went on to say, "I was so much in love with her I couldn't control my desire to see her in person. I've been in love with that girl since I first saw her on the screen in 1936. I figured this was a good way to get to meet her." He was wrong. Instead he got to see the judge again, who cancelled his probation and sent him to jail.

• • •

Betty Grable and Mae West weren't the only stars to be targeted by teens. As 1942 was coming to a close, Errol Flynn found himself in the papers being accused of statutory rape by two seventeen-year-old girls. On November 11, the actor received a letter at his home, reading:

> If you value your life and career, send a small package containing $10,000 in currency to the Otto Malt Shop. Your phone has been tapped so don't call police. You will be killed if you do not comply.
>
> Jack Gilstrom

The Otto Malt Shop was located in San Bernardino, California, and the date given was November 20. The note was turned over to the FBI and a dummy package was left at the malt shop along with some undercover G-Men and San Bernardino police officers. "Jack Gilstrom" turned out to be thirteen-year-old Billy Seamster, who was quickly arrested. The youth told authorities he wanted some spending money and chose Flynn because he'd seen his name in the paper so much lately. He was turned over to his parents.

Marlene Dietrich and her daughter Maria inset with portions of extortion notes.

(L-R) Mae West's chauffer Albert "Chalky" Wright, Investigator Harry Dean, dressed as Mae, Investigator Ray Southard. When extortionists threatened to disfigure Mae, this trio tried unsuccessfully to apprehend them.

Edward Schiffert a.k.a. Richard Harding terrorized Thelma Todd
through the mail for six months before G-Men caught up with him.

G-Men caught sailor James Hall before he could follow
through with any of his threats against Ginger Rogers.

Four

PLUNDERING THE STARS

Home burglaries weren't unheard of in the movie colony, and once again we can look to the Pickford family for an example. On the evening of June 22, 1924, while Jack Pickford was at the beach, thieves climbed through the rear window of his home and stole approximately $40,000 worth of jewelry. Eleven years later, on April 1, 1935, John Gilbert was in his master bathroom when he heard somebody ransacking his bedroom. He walked into the room and scared away a burglar who had cut through the screen of his patio door and entered his abode. The burglar took off, having only managed to snatch the actors .38 pistol.

As it would turn out, the most successful criminal to have preyed on the stars wasn't a bandit, kidnapper, or extortionist but a burglar named Ralph Graham, whose exploits were so successful the press would call him the "Phantom of Bel-Air."

In a crime spree spanning the four years of 1935 to 1939, Graham raided the homes of approximately sixty people in the Hollywood area, a third of whom were such A-listers as Gary Cooper, Barbara Stanwyck, and Carole Lombard, stealing an estimated $2,500,000 in jewelry and other items. Unfortunately for Ralph, he had a greedy fence and only realized about a 1 percent return on the dollar value of the stolen goods. Dissatisfaction with his fence would eventually lead to his downfall.

Graham was born Willard Borton in Gloucester City, New Jersey, at about the turn of the century. When he was a child the family moved to Philadelphia and Borton began his criminal career as a minor. He was arrested the first time at age eleven for "felonious entry and larceny" but the charges were dropped. At thirteen he was caught in a burglary and sent to the Glenn Mills Reformatory, where he served a couple of months before being discharged. Less than a year later he was back for taking part in another burglary. When he was seventeen he was sentenced to sixteen months in the New Jersey State Reformatory.

For the next sixteen years of his life Borton was in and out of prison for various charges. His crimes and punishments weren't limited to New Jersey either; he did time in Jacksonville, Florida; Baltimore; Pittsburgh; and Florence, Arizona, as well as Philadelphia. In July of 1933 he was back in New Jersey and, with a partner named Gentry, went on a safe-cracking spree in Ocean County. For about a month they hit a different business nearly every night before the robberies abruptly stopped.

With his share of the profits Borton began managing a restaurant in Point Pleasant, New Jersey, along with his wife and stepson. Things were quiet until the spring of 1934 when his old partner Gentry was arrested in Philadelphia for transporting stolen cars across state lines. While in custody, Gentry squealed about the safe-cracking business from the previous summer and named Borton as his partner. Jersey police picked up Borton and placed him in the jail at Point Pleasant, and then headed to Philadelphia to interview Gentry. While they were in the City of Brotherly Love getting the lowdown on Borton, their prisoner managed to escape from the Point Pleasant jail. He hurried home, got his wife and stepson, and hightailed it out of town.

On November 21, 1934, six months after Borton and his family disappeared from New Jersey, the body of a nineteen-year-old girl named Ethel Allen was found in Eau Gallie, Florida. According to witnesses, Ethel was last seen leaving a party with a man in a 1929 Ford that had Pennsylvania license plates. Police were able to determine where the guy with the Ford was living and upon arrival questioned an informant. "He's married," they were told. "He lived there with his wife and son. He seemed to have plenty of money and spent most of his time fishing. They moved out on the day Ethel Allen's body was found without saying a word to anyone."

Through a process that wasn't fully disclosed Florida police named Borton as the probable killer and, on December 17, filed a complaint charging Willard Borton with "Unlawfully fleeing from the state of Florida to avoid prosecution for murder." As the Florida authorities went about building their case Borton and his family pulled into Hollywood, California.

A new beginning called for a new name. From here on out Willard Borton was Ralph Graham, and it was as Ralph that he rented a bungalow for his family on Formosa Street. The Grahams were considered friendly but never really got close to their neighbors. They appeared to live comfortably but not flashy. The Grahams enjoyed playing tennis and boating. Ralph also went in for fishing and photography. All these things cost money, however, and by the spring of 1935 Ralph's bankroll was pretty slim. It was time to get back to work.

Still driving his 1929 Ford, Ralph began to cruise the affluent Bel-Air and Brentwood sections of Los Angeles. What he saw appealed to his inner burglar, namely the amazing houses of the wealthy that dotted the region, most set back off the roads surrounded by trees and bushes. Though the landscaping was no doubt meant for privacy, it also provided perfect cover for anyone wanting to conceal himself.

Ralph began his crime spree that April. As a burglar he had some self-imposed rules; he would not knowingly enter a house where there was a child or an elderly woman. "I've got a conscience about kids and old ladies," he would say later. He would also only "work" when the moon shone bright. "I'm kind of superstitious about the moon," he said. "I mean, it's lucky for me and then you don't need a flashlight when you've got the moon to see by. That cuts down the chances of attracting attention."

After an initial robbery of $3,000 worth of jewelry he hit his first movie star, actress Doris Kenyon, on the evening of April 15. In the rear of her house a stairway lead up to a second story balcony perched outside a bedroom. While Doris entertained some guest in her first floor drawing room, Ralph ascended the balcony stairs and let himself in through a French door. While the guest partied downstairs Ralph helped himself to $4,825 worth of Doris's jewelry as well as a few other items.

Ralph's next job of note came on September 17, when he broke into the mansion of food processing tycoon George Hormel. Parking his car a short distance away, Ralph crept up to the house. He tried to jimmy the back door but it was secure. Spying a rose trellis, Ralph climbed up to the master bedroom window and, breaking the glass, let himself in. A short time later he exited the house with a pillow case containing $1,800,000 in stocks and bonds. Since the certificates were registered Ralph wouldn't be able to sell them, so he set them aside and continued with his moonlit raids.

In his expose on the "Phantom of Bel-Air" Captain John Edwards of the L.A.P.D. tells us that one of the houses that Ralph hit after the Hormel job belonged to a "prominent motion picture executive." Most likely he was referring to Darryl F. Zanuck, who would later be listed as a victim. In this case Ralph nabbed $32,000 worth of jewelry and furs.

Just after New Year's 1936 Ralph read an interesting ad in the classified section of the newspaper:

Liberal reward will be paid to party who has found securities taken from home of George Hormel. Must be delivered immediately, otherwise new certificates will be obtained. No questions asked.

Ralph contacted the lawyer whose name was listed in the ad and inquired about the reward. The lawyer refused to answer any questions, stating that he would only speak to whoever possessed the bonds. Ralph hung up and hatched a plan. He took an envelope containing a bond and went to the building where the lawyer's office was located. He went in the men's room outside the office and placed the envelope on top of a towel box. Ralph returned home and called the lawyer back telling him about the envelope.

Once the lawyer was satisfied that he was dealing with the proper party a plan to exchange the bonds for the $2,500 "reward" was put into effect. The first exchange took place in a cigar store. The lawyer approached the counter where there was a package waiting for him. In return he bought something and had the item and the money wrapped and left behind the desk for an H.C. Hart to pick up. Posing as Hart, Ralph collected his money. Three other exchanges like this took place before Hormel had his bonds and Ralph had his twenty-five hundred bucks.

As the illicit funds ran in, Ralph bought a house located at 420 Howland Canal in the town of Venice. Ralph furnished his new abode by the same method he financed it: burglary. He would rent a trailer and pull up to a house and simply break in and take what he wanted. In one instance, at the house belonging to George Theodore, an L.A. laundry owner, Ralph made off with a grand piano. In the case of the Theodores, the laundry owner was in the process of moving so Ralph simply showed up with a trailer and helped himself to a bedroom set, some expensive drapery, and the afore-mentioned piano. Anyone who may have witnessed the theft would have assumed he was a mover.

Ralph also purchased a 36-foot cabin cruiser, which he kept docked at San Pedro. An accessory of the boat, a gaff used to hook swordfish, pulled double duty for Ralph. Not only did he use it for fishing but also for burglary. When he needed access to a second story window but there was no trellis or balcony to climb, he would use the hook to hoist himself up. Police stated that he used this method approximately twenty times before he lost it while pulling a job on May 23, 1937. As Ralph was leaving the house with goods valued at six hundred dollars, the homeowners, Mr. and Mrs. Hilton, surprised him. Mrs. Hilton grabbed the hook while Mr. Hilton made a move against Ralph, who dropped everything and ran away.

That same year saw high-profile jobs pulled by Ralph. On July 30 he hit both Gary Cooper's and Twentieth Century Fox producer Sol Wurtzel's houses. In the case of Cooper's mansion Ralph let himself in by cutting through the screen of a bathroom window. Gary and his wife were out for the evening and a housekeeper was oblivious to his presence, so he had the run of the place. Once inside, he helped himself to jewelry valued at $25,000. While ransacking the actor's bedroom he also helped himself to a pistol. Other valuables taken included a movie camera, radio, and some expensive tableware. The Wurtzels fared better, losing approximately $7,900 in jewelry.

Two weeks later French actress Ketti Gallian returned from a weekend at Santa Barbara to find that Ralph had been there. Jewelry valued at upwards of twenty thousand dollars and six sables worth $1,000 apiece were gone. Also missing was perfume valued at more than a grand. Later that week, on August 20, for some reason never divulged, Ralph returned all her belongings except for the perfume. Gallian was entertaining some friends when her butler interrupted to tell her that he had heard a "suspicious" noise outside. The party went to investigate and on opening the front door they found a suitcase. Gallian called the police, who came to investigate, and when they opened the grip there was all of Gallian's furs and jewelry. "The whole thing is fantastic," the French actress responded when asked about the ordeal.

Not every Hollywood personality that was victimized by Ralph made the press. In fact, six months would pass before one of Ralph's high-profile jobs again made the papers. This time the target was Barbara Stanwyck. On the night of February 25, 1938, Ralph crept up to her house and forced his way through a screen door. Stanwyck was out and while two of her servants slept, Ralph made his way to the star's bedroom where he rifled her dresser and made off with a leather jewel case containing rings, watches, and brooches worth $9,365. Being a fan of the actress, Ralph left a note in her boudoir:

"You have the honor to have as a visitor one of the best.
    K. P. G. G. L. –X for you"

The letters stood for, "Keep plugging good girl love. A kiss for you."

Less than two months after Barbara Stanwyck was robbed, it was Miriam Hopkins's turn. On April 13, she informed the police that $15,000 in jewelry had been snatched from her bedroom closet. Nine nights later Ralph found himself nonchalantly walking about Carole Lombard's mansion. After robbing a nearby neighbor of $18,000 worth of jewels and furs, Ralph managed to let himself in through Ms. Lombard's front door. The star and her live-in secretary were out, so Ralph was able to take his time. He made his way to Lombard's bedroom and helped himself to a jewel-encrusted watch that Clark Gable had given her, as well as the rest of her jewelry, valued at around $21,500. Then he made his way into a room used by Ms. Lombard's secretary, where he helped himself to another $3,500 in jewelry. Once he had the desired baubles in his pocket Ralph made his way downstairs and fixed himself a drink at the bar. He also noticed a nickel slot machine. Retrieving a coin from his pocket, he pressed it into the slot and pulled the lever. He lost. After enjoying his cocktail, he left.

That summer Ralph came face to face with one of his victims. On the night of July 18, Ralph approached the house of director Frank Capra; he climbed to a second-story window and let himself in. The famous director was out but his wife was at home. As Ralph looked about he realized he was inside the bedroom of Capra's young son. Since this violated one of his rules he planned to walk out the front door, but as he was about to enter the hallway he heard somebody coming up the stairs. Pulling out his gun, Ralph stepped into the hallway and met Capra's wife. "If you scream I'll shoot you," he told her. "I was going to rob your house," he continued. "But I saw that baby, so I'm on my way out." As Mrs. Capra stood there, frightened, Ralph ran down the stairs and out the door.

Mrs. Capra aside, the closest Ralph ever came to getting captured on a job came later that year on November 29. He had parked his car near a house that ice-skating star Sonja Henie had been staying in. He gained access to the home but found nothing of value. Not wanting to leave empty handed, he grabbed some canned fish and a clothes iron he found in a closet. He placed the items in a metal wastepaper basket and took them back to his car. The night was young so Ralph went back on the prowl. Still on foot he made his way up the canyon to Maureen O'Sullivan's house. Approaching the back door, Ralph attempted to gain entrance. Ms.

O'Sullivan heard the noise and investigated, scaring Ralph off. The actress immediately called the police while Ralph ran and hid in some bushes. A few minutes later a patrol car arrived so Ralph made his way back down the canyon. He found an abandoned house along the way and hid out while the police patrolled the area. After an hour or so, he headed for his car.

While the O'Sullivan debacle was taking place two private guards had stumbled across Ralph's auto and decided to stake it out. At about 1:30 a.m. Ralph strode up to his car and suddenly there was a flashlight shining on his face, "Put up your hands," a voice demanded. Ralph complied. "Shake him down," said the man holding the light. The other guard frisked Ralph and found the gun he had stolen from Gary Cooper.

The guards wanted to know why he was there. Thinking fast, Ralph told the men that he was hired by the studio as security to keep an eye on Sonja Henie's house. He continued the lie by saying that he had just seen a man go up to the place. The men weren't quite convinced but they didn't want to be responsible for the Henie residence being robbed either, so they escorted Ralph to the back patio. They climbed onto a small wall to get a better look at the house. Suddenly Ralph exclaimed, "Look, there's a man climbing through the window." When the men looked, Ralph leapt from the wall and was disappearing in the darkness before the men could actively give chase. They fired three shots at him but Ralph escaped unscathed. Though he dodged a bullet, both figuratively and literally, Ralph's night was a bust—not only did he have nothing to show for his almost-capture, but he also lost his car. Fortunately, for himself, he had the foresight to register it under a fake name and address.

Four months later Ralph's luck ran out. For the past couple of years the burglar's main fence in Los Angeles was a jeweler named Morris Wasserman, but there was no love lost between the two men. Ralph always felt that Wasserman was ripping him off and so in the summer of 1938 Ralph flew up to San Francisco where he started a relationship with a couple of jewelers named Frank Cator and George Zwillinger. Cator had a record of ten arrests, dating back to 1927. After a home invasion on March 3, 1939, in which Ralph stole about $25,000 worth of jewelry from a family named Woods, he returned to San Francisco on March 22. The following day as he left Cator's jewelry shop and headed for a cab, two detectives approached him and let him know he was under arrest. Ralph made a break for it but was quickly subdued and ended up with a black eye for his troubles. How the detectives learned that Ralph was in town was never divulged.

Once in custody, Ralph asserted that he was a middleman working for a gang of house burglars but soon changed his tune and dropped the lie. His fingerprints proved that he was Willard Borton. Ralph couldn't deny his real identity, but he did deny having anything to do with the murder back in Florida.

San Francisco authorities contacted the Los Angeles police and let them know that they had the probable "Phantom of Bel-Air." Detectives went to Ralph's house and arrested his wife, who tried to escape through a window. While there they were amazed at the amount of stolen items from Ralph's many outings—in addition to the jewelry and furs, there were cameras, projectors, guns, typewriters, musical instruments, and all types of furniture and other furnishings. They also went to his stepson's house, who, now married and living in Santa Barbara, was also arrested after they found a camera and two rings that belonged to Gary Cooper. Normally, underworld sorts live by a no-snitch rule, but Ralph had no problem singing about George Wasserman. "He's as guilty as I am," Ralph said about his Hollywood fence. "And if he hadn't been such a cheap chiseler, I wouldn't be in this spot now."

Ralph was flown back to Los Angeles where members of the press were waiting. Ralph enjoyed his time in the spotlight. "It was easy," he said when asked how he did it. "These motion picture celebrities buy expensive jewelry, wear it a few times, tire of it and then leave it lying around the house. They leave the doors of their homes unlatched at night or ground-floor windows open. I would just walk in and help myself."

He also claimed that the value placed on the things he stole from the stars was inflated. "Most of them exaggerated their losses. Fanny Brice [whom he robbed of jewelry worth $2,825 in October of 1938] told the truth as to the value of her gems." He added, "I didn't know it was her home or I wouldn't have entered it."

When asked if guard dogs were a good measure of prevention he scoffed at the idea, saying that a pocketful of hamburger took care of that. He went on to say the cats actually proved a bigger hindrance. While robbing the home of producer Norman Manning, he found himself being followed around by numerous mewing cats. They got to be such a distraction that he had to go to the kitchen and pour them some milk. The Capra robbery came up. "I lost my nerve right there, for I like kids," he said. "I walked out into the hall and started to leave and there I met Mrs. Capra. I had to threaten her with a gun to get away, but I wouldn't have harmed her."

Detectives took Ralph up on an offer to take a tour of all the houses he had robbed. Hoping to clear up as many unsolved cases as possible, they went off into the rain. Photographers were also on hand. One of the first celebrity homes they stopped at was owned by Tyrone Power, whom Ralph had robbed of $4,000 in jewelry and a large gold crucifix that had been in the family for centuries. They went up to the house and rang the bell. Power's mother answered the door and introductions were made. Mrs. Power asked Ralph if there was any chance of getting the crucifix back. "Where is the cross. I want that back especially."

"I'm afraid it's been melted up for the gold," Ralph replied, "I'm sorry. Terribly sorry. If I can, I'll see where it's gone."

Ralph was then introduced to Tyrone Power and his fiancée, Anabella French. They asked how he managed to break in. Ralph borrowed a penknife and a cigarette case from a detective and in a mere thirteen seconds removed the latch to a patio door. "You'd better triple-lock your doors. And get a burglar alarm they can hear all the way to the city hall," the burglar told the movie star, "Right now a baby could get into your house." The photographers convinced Mr. Power to shake hands with Ralph and pose for a picture. Then they were off.

After the visit with Tyrone Power Ralph's vanity kicked in; he didn't like the fact that he was being photographed with the black eye he received from the San Francisco detectives so the party made a stop at a Hollywood beauty salon, where Frank Factor—son of famous makeup artist Max Factor—covered Ralph's shiner.

The tour continued with stops at Barbara Stanwyck's house and Gary Cooper's abode. "Now there's a good guy." Ralph said, "I'm really sorry I took him, that is if it annoyed him any." They also stopped by Carole Lombard's house and her maid let them in. "That thing's a gyp," Ralph said, pointing out the slot machine that took his nickel. Other than Tyrone Power there were no other movie stars at home, and the tour wrapped up without any further fanfare.

In addition to those already discussed, other Hollywood homes that Ralph targeted included Ann Dvorak, Alice Faye, Fred MacMurray, Lili Damita, and Lila Lee. While discussing his famous victims the fact came up that he hadn't robbed Lupe Velez. "Once I thought about casing her place," he said, "but I didn't because I think her jewelry was junk." This little tidbit was too good for some journalist to pass up so some reporter went to RKO studios where the "Mexican Spitfire" was then filming *The Girl from Mexico* and informed her on what Ralph said and asked for a response. "I'm glad Ralph Graham thinks my jewels are junk," she responded, "But the real reason he didn't rob my house was that the crook's grapevine told him that it is well protected, that I always keep a .45 on hand and can hit what I shoot at.

"I'm not fool enough to leave valuable jewels around where burglars can get them," she continued. "They are in a safe place when I am not wearing them and I am well guarded when I do."

Tyrone Power faced some fallout for posing with Ralph for the press. It was reported that he took some razzing on the set of his film *Second Fiddle*. Fans also were dismayed at why he would do such a thing. Hollywood gossip columnist Louella Parsons came to his defense, informing her readers that:

"Tyrone Power couldn't be more upset over the picture of him shaking hands with Ralph Graham, the "Phantom Burglar." I mentioned to Ty

that my desk was flooded with letters and postcards and the telephone kept ringing asking how a fine young man like Tyrone Power could have shaken hands with a burglar and met with him as well.

Ty explained that when the detectives and cameramen descended on him at breakfast he was so surprised he almost choked on his ham and eggs. One of the photographers begged, "Be a good scout and give us a picture shaking hands with the burglar – it's good human interest stuff." Because he is one of the most obliging actors in Hollywood and always does what is expected of him, Ty posed for the boys without thinking of the consequences."

After the police completed the monumental task of cataloguing all of the items found in Ralph's house, victims who had filed reports and itemized their losses were invited to come and see if they could identify any of their goods. Barbara Stanwyck was unable to find any of her jewelry, but she did come across a camera that Ralph had snatched from her. Carole Lombard's secretary reclaimed a $3,000 brooch, while Mrs. Sol Wurtzel found her jade cigarette case and Fanny Brice's daughter retrieved a bracelet.

In the end Ralph pleaded guilty. At first he was going to plead non-guilty by reason of insanity and go to trial but then he changed his mind. He swore that his wife and stepson had nothing to do with his crimes. There was no evidence to prove otherwise, so they were released. Since this was Ralph's third felony offense, he was given a life sentence without parole and sent to San Quentin to serve out his term. Morris Wasserman later pleaded guilty and was sentenced to serve from one to five years and joined Ralph in San Quentin. San Francisco jewelers Frank Cator and George Zwillinger were subsequently acquitted.

Ralph would end up serving only ten years of his life sentence. On October 11, 1949 he was stabbed to death in the prison barbershop.

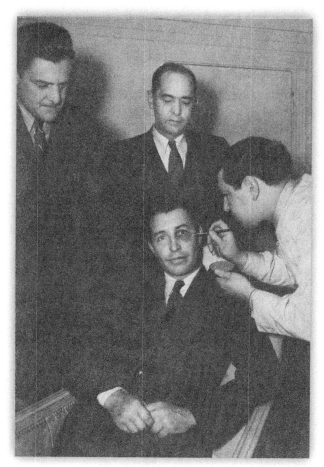

The Phantom of Bel-Air, Ralph Graham, gets the star treatment as a make-up artist works to cover the shiner he received from an arresting detective.

Graham left a personalized letter for Barbara
Stanwyck while robbing her house.

After robbing Carole Lombard's house Graham stuck
around for a cocktail and a try on her slot machine.

Jesse James meets the Phantom: Ralph Graham shakes
hands with victim Tyrone Power at the actor's house. Power
would take much razzing for posing for this shot.

A number of the Phantom's victims peruse some of the loot
police retrieved from Graham's home after his arrest.

Notes

Chapter 1
The Plot to Kidnap America's Sweetheart

<u>Books</u>
Doug and Mary: A Biography of Douglas Fairbanks & Mary Pickford
Gary Carey
E.P. Dutton, 1977

Pickford: The Woman Who Made Hollywood
Eileen Whitfield
The University Press of Kentucky, 1997

Mary Pickford: America's Sweetheart
Scott Eyman
Donald I. Fine, Inc. 1990

Sunshine and Shadow
Mary Pickford
McCall Corporation, 1954

Magazines
Master Detective November 1934
"Smashing the Mary Pickford Kidnapping Plot"
By Harry J. Raymond, former Chief of Detectives, Los Angeles County, California as told to William Dutton Smith

Startling Detective January 1932
"The Inside Story of the Plot to Kidnap Joan Crawford"
By Morton Faber

Newspapers
The Los Angeles Times
"Three Seized In Plot To Kidnap Mary Pickford" 5/31/25
"Three Confess Pickford Plot" 6/1/25
"Kidnaping Pair Ready To Pay" 6/2/25
"Pickford Plot Charges Filed" 6/3/25
"Mary Too Busy To Be In Court" 6/6/25
"Pickford Kidnap Case Up" 7/19/25
"Mary Given Summons In Kidnap Case" 7/21/25
"Pickford Case Set For Today" 7/22/25
"Hunt Pickford Case Witness" 7/23/25
"Pickford Kidnapping Case Goes To Trial With Mary Absent" 7/23/25
"Pickford Case Jury Complete" 7/25/25
"Speed up Pickford Case" 7/27/25
"Pickford Death Plans Charged" 7/28/25
"Transcript of Testimony Offered By Doug At Trial" 7/29/25
"Third-Degree Methods In Pickford Case" 7/29/25
"Crowds Accord "America's Sweetheart" Warm Tribute At Hearing" 7/30/25
"State Fights Pickford Case Brutality Charge" 7/31/25
"Pickford Defense Elated" 8/1/25
"State Closes In Pickford Trial" 8/4/25
"Pickford Dismissal Asked" 8/5/25
"Defense Hit In Pickford Case" 8/6/25

"Kidnap Plot Laid To Geck" 8/7/25
"Pickford Defense Scores" 8/8/25
"Pickford Case Details Given" 8/12/25
"Pickford Plot Duo Guilty" 8/14/25
The New York Times
"Mary Pickford Gets Birthday Gifts" 4/8/25
"See Plot To Kidnap Mary Pickford" 5/31/25
"Three Confess in Pickford Plot" 6/1/25
"Crowd Hears Story of Mary Pickford" 7/30/25
The Port Arthur News
"Mary Pickford Employs Double Who Protects Her From Dangers of Life" 6/10/25
The North Adams Transcript
"Plot To Kidnap Mary Pickford Is Frustrated" 6/1/25
The Capital Times
"Target of Kidnap Plot" 7/24/31
The Era Bradford PA.
"Bares Kidnap Plot" 7/24/31
The Laredo Times
"Fairbanks Kidnap Probe is Dropped" 7/27/31
Los Angeles Times
"Ann Harding's Daughter Under Constant Guard"

Ancestry.com
California, Prison and Correctional Records, 1851-1950

Chapter 2
Stick 'Em Up

Books
Mae West George Eells and Stanley Musgrove, William Morrow & Company, 1982

She Always Knew How: Mae West, a Personal Biography, Charlotte Chandler, Simon & Schuster, 2009

Magazines
Startling Detective, November 1936
"Fame Points the Finger"
By Joseph Csida, Jr.

True Detective Mysteries, November 1934
"They Done Her Wrong" – Crushing the Mae West Extortion Plot
By Detective Lieutenant S.S. Stone L.A.P.D as told to Madeline Kelley

Newspapers
Chicago Tribune
Tex Guinan, Queen of Whoopee! 3/4/51
Oakland Tribune
Male Sleuth Doubles for Mae West But Curves Fail to Lure Suspect 10/8/35
Los Angeles Times
Mae West Gem Quiz Traps Two 12/5/33
Mae West To Take Stand 1/15/34
Police Guard Mae West 1/16/34
Mae Steals Court Scene 1/17/34
Guards Sent To Mae West 1/25/34
Friedman Sentenced in Mae West Jewel Robbery Case 2/15/34
Mae West Leads Stars In War On Gangsters 3/11/34
Officers Capture Mae West Death Threat Suspect 10/8/35
New Arrests In Mae West Threat Near 10/9/35
West Case Youth Free 10/10/35
Harry Voiler Exonerated in Robbery of Mae West 3/17/38
New York Times
Mae West Robber Guilty 2/4/34

www.TCM.com

Production notes for *Night After Night, She Done Him Wrong, Belle of The Nineties.*

<u>Newspapers</u>

McDermott robbery – The Bakersfield Californian 4/6/25

Lottie Pickford robbery –
    Steubenville Herald-Star 11/10/28
    Appleton Post-Crescent 11/10/28
    Evening Sun, Hanover, PA. 11/10/28

Douglas Fairbanks robbery – Los Angeles Times 8/4/30

Helene Costello robbery – Los Angeles Times 10/21/32

Betty Compson robbery –
    The Billings Gazette 1/8/33
    Charleston Gazette 1/7/33
    The Salt Lake Tribune 1/6/33
    The Sheboygan Press 1/6/33
    The Tipton Daily Tribune 1/17/33
    Joplin Globe 1/17/33

Aileen Pringle robbery –
    Ironwood Daily Globe 2/2/33
    Oakland Tribune 2/2/32
    San Mateo Times 2/2/33
    Nevada State Journal 2/2/33

Zeppo Marx robberies –
    New York Times 8/23/32
    New York Times 6/2/33

Chapter 3

Shaking Down Tinseltown

Books
King of Comedy
Mack Sennett
Garden City: Doubleday, 1954

Marlene Dietrich
Maria Riva
First Ballantine Books, 1992

Marlene
Marlene Dietrich
Grove Press, 1989

Blue Angel: The Life of Marlene Dietrich
Donald Spoto
Doubleday, 1992

Marlene: The Life of Marlene Dietrich
Charles Higham
W.W. Norton & Company, 1977

Marlene Dietrich: Life & Legend
Steven Bach
William Morrow & Co., 1992

The Life and Death of Thelma Todd
William Donati
McFarland, 2012

Ginger: My Story
Ginger Rogers
Harper Collins Publishers, 1991

Magazines
Photoplay, February 1937
"Ginger Was Threatened with Death"
By Kay Proctor

Startling Detective, November 1936
"Fame Points the Finger"
By Joseph Csida, Jr.

Front Page Detective, April 1937
"Hollywood Shakedown"
By Mark Thomas

True Detective, March 1936
"The Unpublished Truth About the Thelma Todd Extortion Case"
By Andrew J. Viglietta

Inside Detective, April 1936
"Was Thelma Todd Murdered?"
By Bruce L. Bolton

Newspapers
Bluefield Daily Telegraph
"Held For Sending Poison Pen Letter To Lew Cody" 1/2/27
Independent, Helena, Montana
"Alleged Blackmailer Held In California" 1/2/27
Appleton Post Crescent
"Mabel Normand! And Lew Cody Married" September 17, 1926

The Bakersfield Californian
"Note Threaten Lew Cody's Life" January 4, 1927
"Thelma Todd Under Guard; Threatened" 3/6/35
"Shirley Temple Receives Threat" 8/1/36
Chester Times, Chester, PA.
"Death Notes Name Film Star's Child" 6/3/32
Los Angeles Times
Film Terrorist Gang Trap Set 10/14/32
Kidnapping Threats Constant in Hollywood; Guarding of Children Costly for Movie Stars 5/8/33
Baby Kidnap Threats Change Bing Crosby's Life 4/15/34
Kidnap Threats Force Screen Stars to Convert Homes Into Forts Patrolled by Guards 5/12/34
Mystery Extortionist Threatens Miss Todd 3/6/35
New Alarm In Todd Case 3/7/35
Threat Sent by Extortioner 8/19/35
Actress Happy as Threat Notes Cease 8/30/35
Officers Capture Mae West Death Threat Suspect 10/8/35
New Arrests In Mae West Threat Near 10/9/35
West Case Youth Free 10/10/35
Suspect in Judy Garland Kidnap Threat Calls Own Account of Ransom Plot Untrue 3/9/40
Betty Grable Extortion Confession Announced 1/4/41
Errol Flynn Victim of Plot 11/20/42
Suspect Seized in Betty Grable Death Threats 3/20/43

New York Times
Seized as Writer Of Extortion Notes 11/8/35
Seized For Threat To Ginger Rogers 12/6/36
Miami News Record
Police Guard Home of Richard Arlen 10/13/32

Brooklyn Daily Eagle
A Columnist, In Hollywood, Sits Down, and Thinks it Over 10/13/32
New Castle News
Guards Surround Thelma Todd's Home 3/6/35
Joplin Globe
Shirley Temple Extortion Plot Confessed by Youth 8/1/36
Beatrice Daily Sun
"Threatens Shirley" 8/3/36
Ukiah Republican Press
Shirley Here On Thursday 8/5/36
The Lowell Sun
Atlanta Youth Held In Kidnap Plot 9/16/36
Syracuse Herald
G-Men Seize U.S. Seaman In Extortion 12/6/36
Ogden Standard Examiner
Extortion Note Lands Youth In F.B.I. Custody 1/4/41
Creston News Advertiser
Betty Grable Again Extortion Victim 2/5/41
The Amarillo Daily News
'Grable Extortioner' Guilty 2/28/41
Evening Times, Cumberland, MD.
Note Writer To Betty Grable On Probation 4/24/41
The Times And Daily News Leader – San Mateo, Calif.
Boy Trapped in Extortion Plot 3/20/43
Waterloo Daily Courier
His Efforts to Meet Film Star Cost Five Years 5/2/43
Mexia Weekly
Boy Held on Extortion Charge Says He Just Wanted to See Movie Stars 4/2/43
Dunkirk (N.Y.) Evening Examiner
La Grable's Admirer Faces Pen Sentence 5/20/43

Chapter 4

Plundering the Stars

Magazines
Headline Detective, July 1939
"The Phantom of Bel-Air"
By John Alexander

True Detective Mysteries, November 1939
"Hollywood's Cat-Man and the Plundered Stars"
By Captain John R. Edwards, Los Angeles Police Department, as told to
M. Kelley Arnold

Newspapers
Los Angeles Times
Phantom Thief Suspect Seized 3/24/39
$1,800,00 Bond Theft Nets $2500 3/26/39
Society Thief Faces Victims 3/27/39
Bel-Air Phantom Identified as Hunted 'Hook' Burglar 3/30/39
Phantom Links Two Jewelers 6/23/39
Bel-Air Thief Given Life 5/19/39
San Antonio Light
Hollywood's Incredible Phantom Burglar 5/7/39
The Kansas City Star
Gem Thief Is A "Softy" 3/26/39
New York Times
Stanwyck Gems Stolen 2/27/38
Miriam Hopkins's Gems Stolen 4/14/38
Film Celebrities Robbed 7/31/37
'Phantom got $2,500 For $1,800,00 Bonds 3/26/39
Oakland Tribune

Gem Burglar Suspect Taken 3/24/39
Film Stars Easy To Rob Says Suspect 3/25/39
Tyrone Power Gets Tip From Burglar 3/27/39
The Ogden Standard-Examiner
Graham Visits Victims' Homes 3/28/39
Actress Gets Camera Back From Phantom 4/4/39
The Yuma Daily Sun and Arizona Sentinel
Pair Acquitted 9/29/39
Lawrence Daily Journal – World
Investigation Broadened 3/25/39
Berkeley Daily Gazette
Report "Raffles" Also Wanted on Murder Charge 3/24/39
Two Win Freedom In Stolen Gem Quiz 3/29/39
The Bristol Courier
Behind the Scenes in Hollywood 4/5/39

About the Author

Patrick Downey specializes in Prohibition era and Depression era crime. His other books include: *Legs Diamond: Gangster*, *Gangster City: The History of the New York Underworld 1900-1935*, and *Bad Seeds in the Big Apple: Bandits, Killers, and Chaos in New York City, 1920-1940*. He can be found on line at deadgangster.blogspot.com

Index

Made in the USA
Las Vegas, NV
30 July 2024

93166571R00066